Elaine Walker
Steve Elsworth

New Edition

Grammar Practice

for Upper Intermediate Students

with key

Pearson Education Limited
Edinburgh Gate
Harlow
Essex CM20 2JE
England
And Associated Companies throughout the World.

www.longman.com

ISBN 0 582 41721 X
Sixth impression 2005
Set in Slimbach

Printed by Spain by Mateu Cromo

Tests on pages 173-184 by Dorothy E. Zemach.

Illustrations by Gillian Martin, Chris Pavely, Ivana Svabic and Celia Witchard.

Designed by Linemead

Project Managed by Lewis Lansford

Contents

To the Student

Grammar Practice for Upper Intermediate Students gives thorough explanations of all the main areas of English grammar and provides exercises for you to do.

This book can be used in class with help from your teacher or at home as a self-study book.

If you are using the book by yourself, use the Index and the Contents list to find the area that you want to study, read the grammatical explanation and then do the exercise. To check your answers, look in the Key.

We hope that *Grammar Practice for Upper Intermediate Students* helps you to improve your English.

Elaine Walker
Steve Elsworth

Nouns, adjectives and adverbs

1 Countable and uncountable nouns

Uncountable nouns

- Names of substances (materials, liquids, gases, etc.):

leather	paper	wood	metal	silver
water	coffee	air	bread	meat
butter	wine	flour		

- Activities and sports:

running	swimming	shopping
gardening	football	tennis
snooker	squash	badminton

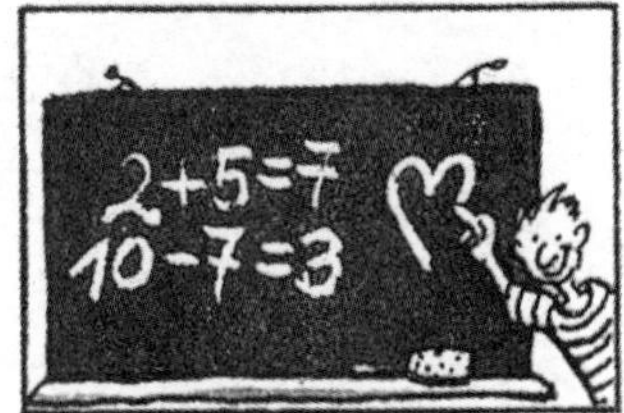

- Names of subjects:

history	mathematics	music
physics	law	art

- Languages:

Russian	Greek	German	English

- Abstract nouns:

love	hope	advice	information
intelligence	beauty	hunger	
poverty			

- Collective nouns:

furniture	luggage	equipment
accommodation	traffic	

Practice

1a Underline all the uncountable nouns in the following text.

We welcome you as a guest at the Sherwood Holiday Village and hope that you enjoy your holiday with us.

The sports complex is open from 7 a.m. and facilities are available for tennis, squash, bowling, table tennis and snooker.

You can hire equipment at the complex for a nominal fee. If you require tuition, there is coaching available but you must book in advance. For those of you who enjoy competition, there will be tournaments taking place throughout the week. Please sign your name up on the notice board if you are interested. And if you need something to quench your thirst after an energetic game, you can purchase fruit juice, mineral water and herbal drinks as well as a variety of healthy snacks from the health-food bar. May we take this opportunity to inform you that appropriate footwear must be worn for all activities and heavy shoes are not allowed in the sports complex.

Next to the sports complex, you will find our brand-new swimming pool, complete with water slides and a wave machine. The lighting in the pool area gives the effect of sunlight even on the dullest days. And if you want to look your best in the pool, our sports shop stocks a wide range of designer swimwear.

After lots of exercise, you'll probably be ready for a good meal. Why not go to the Sherwood Restaurant? If you'd like to try the buffet, you can eat as much food as you like for just £8. If you'd prefer to eat in, you can purchase your food from the minimarket. Fresh fruit and vegetables are delivered to the minimarket daily and the bread is freshly baked by our own bakers.

If you require any advice or information, please come to the Reception Desk and we will be glad to assist.

Janice Hughes, Manager

Nouns which may be uncountable or countable

Many nouns which are generally uncountable can also be countable in certain contexts.

- Some nouns are uncountable when we talk about the substance, material or abstract concept but countable when we talk about one specific item:
  chicken/a chicken, light/a light, stone/a stone, hope/a hope, education/an education, hair/a hair

  *I'm very interested in **education**.*
  *It is important that she receives **a** good **education**.*

  *There isn't much **light** in this room.*
  *Is there **a light** in this room?*

- Some nouns which are uncountable when we talk about the material and countable when we refer to a specific thing have a particular meaning as countable nouns. For example, *glass* refers to a material. *A glass* refers to an item that we drink from which is made of glass. It does not refer to a piece of glass:
  wood/a wood, paper/a paper, iron/an iron, cloth/a cloth

- Some nouns which are usually uncountable can be countable when we refer to a particular variety:
  wine/an excellent wine, cheese/a strong cheese, fruit/a very sweet fruit

- In informal English, drinks and some types of food which are normally uncountable can be counted, particularly when we are making an order in a cafe or restaurant:
  tea/three teas, coffee/a coffee, soup/two soups

- Some ***ing*** forms can be countable:
  painting/a good painting, drawing/a few drawings

Practice

1b Write ***a*** before the nouns which are being used as countable nouns.

1 a) ..–.. Beauty is subjective.

  b) She's .a.. real beauty.

2 a) I am fortunate to have had ..... very good education.

  b) ..... education does not just take place at school.

3 a) My eyes are very sensitive to ..... light.

  b) Is there ..... light in there?

4 a) You've been ..... great help to me.

  b) I'm sorry to ask you but I desperately need ..... help.

5 a) I don't usually drink ..... coffee.

  b) I'll have two teas and ..... coffee please.

6 a) He has ..... great love of music.

  b) Sometimes ..... love can be very painful.

7 a) You'll get better at the job as you gain ..... experience.
  b) I'm so glad I did it: it was ..... wonderful experience.
8 a) The house is built of ..... stone.
  b) This is ..... beautiful stone.
9 a) ..... death comes to us all one day.
  b) There's been ..... death in the family.
10 a) ..... fear is a perfectly natural human feeling.
  b) He has ..... terrible fear of heights.
11 a) He was so hungry that he ate ..... whole chicken.
  b) I don't like red meat but I do eat ..... chicken.
12 a) I think that's ..... really ugly painting.
  b) ..... painting can be a very relaxing activity.
13 a) I usually eat ..... fruit for breakfast.
  b) That's ..... very unusual fruit. What is it?
14 a) Has this soup got ..... potato in it?
  b) Would you like ..... baked potato?
15 a) You shouldn't drink ..... wine on an empty stomach.
  b) This is ..... very nice wine.

2 The article

The indefinite article *a* or *an*

- ***a*** or ***an***? We use ***a*** before consonant sounds and ***an*** before vowel sounds. But note:
  ***a** uniform* /ju:/ ***a** European* /ju:/ ***an** MP* /em/ ***an** L-plate* /el/

USE

We can use the indefinite article before singular countable nouns: we cannot use it before uncountable nouns:
*I bought **a** chair* but NOT ~~*I bought a furniture*~~.

We use the indefinite article:
- when we are referring to one thing but it is not one in particular:
  *I'd like **a** banana.*
- when we refer to something for the first time. With the second reference, we use ***the***:
  *There's **a** man at the door. I think it's **the** man from the garage.*

- after ***to be*** and ***have got*** when we are describing someone or something, including someone's job:
  *She's **a** headteacher.*
  (BUT *She's **the** headteacher of Park School.*)
  *He's got **a** lovely smile.*
  *It's **a** nice day.*
  (BUT *It's **the** nicest day we've had all week.*)
- with a unit of measurement (weight, quantity, time):
  *£2 **a** kilo, three times **a** day, once **a** week*
- In exclamations:
  *What **a** lovely day!*

The definite article: *the*

USE

We can use the definite article before singular and plural countable nouns and before uncountable nouns.

We use it when we are referring to a specific thing or things. This includes:

- when the content of the sentence specifies which particular one(s) we are talking about:
  ***The** people next door have invited us round for a drink.*
  *I'll wear **the** dress I bought last week.*
- when something is referred to for a second time and therefore becomes specific:
  *They've got a boy and a girl. **The** girl's at university now.*
- when we refer to a particular place, person, animal or thing and the speaker and listener know which one(s) is/are being referred to:
  ***The** window cleaner's here.*
  (our regular window cleaner)
  *I think your keys are in **the** kitchen.*
  (our kitchen or the kitchen here)
- when there is only one:
  ***the** world* ***the** sun* ***the** weather* ***the** American Civil War*
- before some collective nouns referring to a whole group of people, including names of nationalities and political parties or groups:
  ***the** British* ***the** Italians* ***the** Conservatives* ***the** police* ***the** government*
  ***the** public* ***the** army* ***the** management* ***the** electorate* ***the** fire brigade*
- before some adjectives (used without a noun) to refer to the group in general:
  ***the** rich* ***the** poor* ***the** unemployed* ***the** disabled*
- before parts of the day:
  *in **the** morning/**the** afternoon/**the** evening*
- before names of ships, newspapers and magazines and some names of musical groups:
  ***The** National Union of Teachers* ***The** QE2* ***The** Daily Mirror* ***The** Economist*
  ***The** Berlin Philharmonic Orchestra*

- before superlatives and ordinals:
  *It's **the** best film I've seen.*
  *That's **the** third time she's phoned.*
- before names of musical instruments when we talk about playing them:
  *Can you play **the** piano?*
  (BUT *I've just bought **a** piano.*)
- before names of seas, rivers, groups of islands, islands called 'The Isle of ...', chains of mountains, deserts, regions and a few names of countries:
  ***the** Atlantic Ocean* ***the** River Nile* ***the** Himalayas* ***the** Sahara*
  ***the** Southern Hemisphere* ***the** Arctic* ***the** north, south,* etc. ***the** USA*
  ***the** Netherlands* ***the** Sudan* ***the** United Arab Emirates* ***the** Ivory Coast*
  ***the** Philippines* ***the** Bahamas* ***the** Isle of Wight*

The zero article (no article)

USE

We do not use an article before plural nouns and singular uncountable nouns when we use them in a general sense.

	Singular countable nouns	*Singular uncountable nouns*	*Plural nouns*
Definite use	**the**	**the**	**the**
Indefinite use	**a/an**	zero article	zero article

Books are very important to me.
*Have you read **the** books I brought you last month?*
Water is the best thing to drink when you're thirsty.
*Did you put **the** water in the fridge?*

Other uses of the zero article:

- with proper nouns:
  Helen's gone to Paris.
  I'm going away on Friday.
- with meals:
  Have you had breakfast yet?
  (BUT *That was **a** lovely breakfast.*)
- with *school, class, college, university, home, work, church, bed, hospital, prison, town* when we talk about going to these places or being in them for their normal use:
  Danny's gone to bed.
  She's been in hospital for three weeks.
  (BUT *There isn't **a** hospital in **the** town.*)
- with ***by*** + item of transport:
  Did you go by train?
- with ***next/last*** + *week, days of the week,* etc:
  next Wednesday, last night, next time

Practice

2a Complete the sentences with ***a*** or ***an***, ***the*** or no article.

1 'How much are ..the.. leeks?' 'They're 80 pence ..a.. pound.'
2 I went to .... wonderful concert by .... London Symphony Orchestra.
3 .... local school is soon to be closed.
4 I usually go to .... work by .... train.
5 Is .... meat in .... oven?
6 Is this .... first time you've been to .... Isle of Man?
7 He's .... art teacher and she's .... electrician.
8 A lot of people give .... money to .... charity at this time of year.
9 What .... beautiful face that child's got!
10 .... British usually have .... butter on their bread.
11 .... life is very difficult for .... unemployed these days.
12 .... Leader of .... Opposition is in danger of losing her seat at .... next election.
13 I like to have .... cup of .... tea when I wake up in .... morning.
14 I saw .... fox this morning. I think it must have been .... same one that I saw last week.
15 Can I have .... apple?
16 Have you ever seen .... Acropolis in .... Athens?
17 .... police have had a lot of support from .... general public over this issue.
18 .... shirts on .... washing-line should be nearly dry now.
19 .... people don't like him because of his selfish attitude.
20 I bought my sister .... book and .... bottle of .... perfume for her birthday but I don't think she liked .... perfume.

2b Put ***a*** or ***an***, ***the*** or no article in the gaps in this letter.

Dear [1]....–.... Jo and Ian,

This is [2]....a.... picture of [3]......... hotel we're staying at. We were lucky enough to get one of [4]......... rooms overlooking [5]......... sea and [6]......... view is lovely. We had [7]......... good journey over here and [8]......... children quite enjoyed [9]......... flight. They've got [10]......... lovely room of their own and they think [11].........

hotel's great. In general, we've all been having [12]......... really good time. Unfortunately, Penny got [13]......... very sunburnt back on [14]......... first day so she's had to wear [15]......... T-shirt since then, but apart from that everyone's been fine. Jeremy's met [16]......... English boy of about [17]......... same age and they get on very well. They went into [18]......... town on their own [19]......... last night and bought themselves [20]......... meal. And tonight they want to go out to [21]......... disco – there are plenty to choose from here.

We've spent most of our time on [22]......... beach so far. [23]......... sea is really warm and clear so we've done lots of [24]......... swimming. Tomorrow we're going on [25]......... boat trip to one of [26]......... islands and we're going to have [27]......... barbecue on [28]......... island. I'm really looking forward to that.

Anyway, I'll give you [29]......... ring when we get back and we'll see you [30]......... next week.

Best wishes,

Sally and Robin

2c Rewrite the reference below in your notebook, adding the definite article ***the*** and the indefinite article ***a*** or ***an*** where appropriate.

Packard Brown Ltd, Digby Industrial Estate, Silton, Bristol BS12 2PE

Reference: Timothy Harding

Timothy Harding has worked for this company for ten years. Throughout this time he has shown himself to be hard-working and enthusiastic employee. He first joined company as junior sales representative but was soon promoted and is now at head of successful team of sales representatives. He manages team with skill and energy and significant increase in sales achieved by team is measure of his success. He has considerable initiative and this has been particularly evident in area of training, where he has had notable success. Training programme he devised for his team has now been adopted throughout company with very positive results.

On personal level, I have found Timothy to be very honest and considerate person and he is well-liked in company. I have no hesitation in recommending him for job for which he has applied, though I would of course be sorry to lose him.

Claire Alexander

Ms Claire Alexander
Director of Personnel

Example: *Timothy Harding has worked for this company for ten years. Throughout this time he has shown himself to be a hard-working and enthusiastic employee. ...*

3 Adjectives

Attributive and predicative adjectives

- When an adjective comes before a noun, it is attributive:
  *She's an **intelligent young** woman.*
  *I love **strong** cheese.*
- When an adjective is separated from the noun and comes after the verb, it is predicative. An adjective can follow verbs like *be, become, get, seem, appear, feel, smell, look, sound, taste, make* (+ person), *keep, stay, grow, turn*. It is a complement of the verb and not an object:
  *The exam was really **difficult**.*
  *She seems **worried**.*
  *Hilary made me very **angry**.*
- A few adjectives can have a different meaning as attributive adjectives from their meaning as predicative adjectives:
  *Jenny's a really **old** friend.*
  (I've known her for a long time.)
  *Margaret's quite **old** now.*
  (old in age)

  *You're a very **heavy** sleeper.*
  (You sleep very heavily; you do not wake up easily.)
  *This suitcase is really **heavy**.*

  *His **late** father used to run the shop.*
  (His father is dead now.)
  *He's nearly always **late**.*
- A few adjectives can be used only as attributive adjectives or only as predicative adjectives:

  Only predicative
  - Some adjectives relating to health, including ***ill***, ***poorly***, ***well/unwell***, ***fine***:
    *She's very **ill**.*
  - Adjectives beginning with a, including ***asleep***, ***awake***, ***afraid***, ***alive***, ***alone***:
    *Do you feel **afraid**?*
  - Some adjectives describing feelings, including ***content***, ***glad***, ***pleased***, ***sorry***, ***upset***: *He seems **upset**.*
  - ***near***, ***far*** (***away***): *It's not **far away**.*

  Only attributive
  - Adjectives which qualify the noun, including ***chief***, ***main***, ***only***, ***particular***, ***principal***, ***sole***: *You're my **only** friend.*

Order of adjectives

When there is more than one adjective preceding a noun, they are generally placed in the following order:

What is it like?	*How big?*	*How old?*	*What shape?*	*What colour?*	*Where was it made?*	*What is it made from?/ What type is it?*	*Noun*
				red	Chinese	silk	shirt
beautiful		old					house
old-fashioned						handmade	doll
	small		square	brown			envelope
	heavy		oval			antique	table

Notes

- ***great big*** generally goes before any other adjectives: *a* ***great big*** *lovely old building.*
- When you use more than one adjective from the *What is it like?* category, it does not usually matter what order they go in:
  She's a ***depressed, anxious*** *young woman.*
  She's an ***anxious, depressed*** *young woman.*
  If one of the adjectives is more general, it is likely to come first:
  It was a ***beautiful, thought-provoking*** *film.*
- We generally only use commas between attributive adjectives when there are two or more adjectives of equal importance describing what something is like. The comma separates the adjectives of equal emphasis. There is often another adjective describing age or type before the noun:
  He's an ignorant, *selfish old man.*
- We can also use ***and*** to separate two attributive adjectives describing what something is like:
  It's a violent ***and*** *shocking book.*
- If we use two adjectives predicatively, we separate the adjectives with ***and***. If there are more than two adjectives, we separate the last two adjectives with ***and*** and the preceding adjectives with a comma:
  He is always bright ***and*** *cheerful.*
  The new teacher is committed, enthusiastic ***and*** *hard-working.*

Practice

3a Rewrite the sentences, putting the words into the correct order. If you think there should be a comma, add it in the correct place.

1 absolutely holiday wonderful was the.

The holiday was absolutely wonderful.

2 enormous they old staying building grey are an in.

....

....

3 and looks now old he tired rather.

....

4 young met student charming we medical a.

....

5 angry an man is young he aggressive.

....

6 heavy is a he smoker very.

....

7 very has happy him she made.

....

8 heavy her gold a gave necklace he beautiful.

....

....

9 close are friends extremely they.

....

10 moment at rather seem the unhappy you.

....

11 thoughtful a be man young seems very he to

....

....

12 impractical is time-wasting expensive the and project.

....

....

13 beginning hair grey turn to is my.

....

14 young actress a Diana successful well-respected and is.

....

....

15 fine am now feeling I.

....

Construction of adjectives

Participles as adjectives

- Many present participles and past participles can be used as adjectives:
  *an **exciting** trip* *a **falling** tree*
  *a **crying** child* *a **completed** manuscript*
  *a **torn** shirt* ***frozen** vegetables*
- Many compound adjectives are formed with participles. ***Well*** + past participle is particularly common:
  *a **well-built** house* ***well-cooked** meat*
  *a **time-wasting** activity* ***handmade** tools*
  *a **fast-selling** product* ***home-grown** vegetables*

Practice

3b Complete the sentences with participles as adjectives, using the verbs in the box. The verbs with adverbs should be used to form compound adjectives.

dry	change	~~act well~~	keep beautifully	break	decline fast
steal	tailor beautifully	bring up well	continue	love	
brush well	~~relax~~	think clearly	park	write well	embarrass
build well	plan badly	boil			

1 It was a very restful holiday so I feel much more ..*relaxed*.. now.

2 It was a very ..*well-acted*.. play.

3 I kept calling her by the wrong name; it was very ....

4 The .... kettle filled the kitchen with steam.

5 She's a very .... child: she always behaves herself well.

6 I think he may have died of a .... heart.

7 Her hair is always very ....

8 The increase in divorce reflects a .... attitude to marriage and relationships.

9 She's a very good person to have in meetings as she's very ....

10 Shortage of money is a .... problem for them: it probably always will be.

11 The house is old but it's very ....

12 It was a .... escape and so it inevitably failed.

13 Badgers are a .... species in this country as more of them are killed every year.

14 That's a .... suit he's wearing.

15 I need some .... fruit to put in the cake.

16 This is a .... garden: someone must spend a lot of time working on it.

17 It was a very .... article.

18 The police may charge you with receiving .... goods.

19 They're a very .... family and they give each other a lot of support.

20 Children should not play near .... cars.

Suffixes and prefixes

Many adjectives have suffixes or prefixes. Some of the more common suffixes are:

- ***-able/ible*** (able to be): *comfort**able**, enjoy**able***
- ***-ful*** (full of, having): *truth**ful**, beauti**ful***
- ***-less*** (being without, not having): *care**less**, power**less***
- ***-ive*** (tending to, having the nature or quality of doing this): *attract**ive**, impuls**ive***

Practice

3c Complete the following sentences with an adjective formed from one of the verbs or nouns in the box, plus a suffix.

act	care	change	comfort	describe	dread	~~enjoy~~	
forget	grace	motion	power	rely	submit	tire	truth

1 We had a lovely weekend; it was thoroughly .enjoyable.. .
2 He never remembers my birthday; I don't know why he's so ....
3 The problem is that there's nothing we can do about it; we're completely ....
4 I believe what he says because he's always been .... in the past.
5 She never seems to run out of energy; she's completely ....
6 She's a very .... writer; she gives you a very good feel for the places and characters in her stories.
7 Don't worry. If he's said he'll be there, then I sure he will. He's very ....
8 His problem is that he always does exactly what people tell him to do: he's just so ....
9 You're so ....: you're always dropping things.
10 I love to watch good ballet dancers: they're so ....
11 The cat stayed .... as it waited to pounce on the bird.
12 It's a very .... climate; the weather can be completely different from one day to the next.
13 It's important to keep .... after you retire.
14 The seats in first class were really .... I could easily have fallen asleep in them.
15 The situation out there is .... More and more people are dying every day.

Negative prefixes

There are a number of negative prefixes including the following:

- ***dis-*** ***dis**agreeable* ***dis**honest*
- ***un-*** ***un**interesting* ***un**necessary*
- ***il-*** ***il**legal* ***il**logical*
- ***im-*** ***im**possible* ***im**polite*
- ***in-*** ***in**convenient* ***in**significant*
- ***ir-*** ***ir**responsible* ***ir**relevant*

Practice

3d Copy the table into your notebook and put the adjectives in the box into the correct columns.

~~patient~~ relevant attractive literate flexible regular legal
agreeable mature convenient tasteful moral replaceable
responsible significant possible legible honest rational
explicable justified mortal reversible destructible perfect
friendly soluble polite logical interesting separable

dis-	*un-*	*il-*	*im-*	*in-*	*ir-*
			impatient		

Non-gradable adjectives

A non-gradable adjective is one that cannot be qualified by words like *very, too* and *enough.*

Non-gradable adjectives include words like:
***weekly*, *unconscious*, *dead*, *legal*, *medical*, *empty*, *full*.**
where the meaning is strictly defined and cannot be qualified. There are, for example, no degrees of being dead or unconscious. Thus we cannot say '~~*very dead*~~'.

Other non-gradable adjectives are adjectives with a very strong meaning like:
***wonderful*, *perfect*, *terrible*, *astonished*, *delicious*, *amazing*, *hilarious*.**
Astonished*,** for example, already means *very/extremely/completely surprised*, and so we cannot say 'very astonished'. But we can add some strength to these words by preceding them with ***absolutely or ***really***:
***absolutely** wonderful*
***really** amazing*

Practice

3e Copy the table into your notebook and write the adjectives in the correct columns. Put them into pairs of adjectives with similar meanings.

~~surprising~~ starving nice filthy devastated wonderful
hungry delicious big tasty furious ugly impossible
small hideous terrified good enormous tired thirsty
~~amazing~~ angry vital parched dirty upset important
terrible frightened minute exhausted perfect difficult
bad

Gradable	*Non-gradable*
surprising	amazing

4 Comparison of adjectives

	Comparative	*Superlative*
One-syllable adjectives: young, big, short	young**er**, bigg**er**, short**er**	young**est**, bigg**est**, short**est**
Two-syllable adjectives ending in -y: lovely, pretty, funny	loveli**er**, pretti**er**, funni**er**	loveli**est**, pretti**est**, funni**est**
Other two-syllable adjectives: pleasant, annoyed, modern, careful careless	**more** pleasant **more** annoyed **more** modern **more** careful **more** careless	**most** pleasant **most** annoyed **most** modern **most** careful **most** careless
Adjectives of three or more syllables: expensive, attractive, exciting, intelligent	**more** expensive **more** attractive **more** exciting **more** intelligent	**most** expensive **most** attractive **most** exciting **most** intelligent
Adjectives with irregular comparatives and superlatives: good, bad, far	**better**, **worse**, **further/farther**	**best**, **worst**, **furthest/farthest**

Notes

- ***Less*** and ***least*** can be used in comparative and superlative sentences:
  *Travelling by train is **less** tiring than driving.*
  *This must be the **least** attractive part of the coast.*

  Least is sometimes used in the expression '*not in the **least***' meaning 'not at all':
  *It doesn't matter **in the least** if you can't come. I'll see you next week.*

- Spelling:

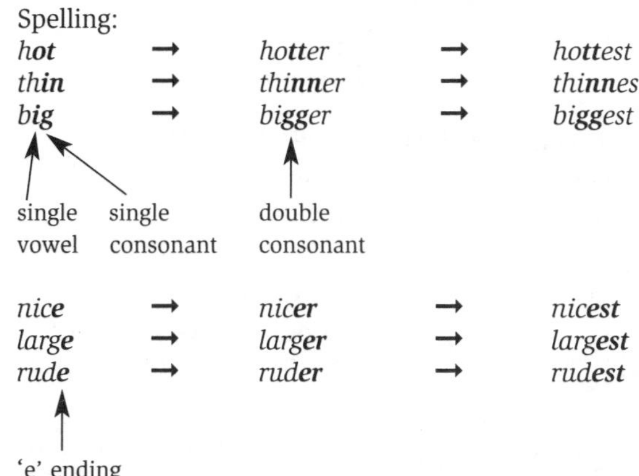

  nice → *nic**er*** → *nic**est***
  *larg**e*** → *larg**er*** → *larg**est***
  *rud**e*** → *rud**er*** → *rud**est***
  'e' ending

- An adjective with a negative prefix forms its comparative and superlative in the same way as the adjective without the negative prefix:

kind → *kind**er*** → *kind**est***	***un**kind* → ***un**kind**er*** → ***un**kind**est***
happy → *happ**ier*** → *happ**iest***	***un**happy* → ***un**happ**ier*** → ***un**happ**iest***
honest → ***more** honest* → ***most** honest*	***dis**honest* → ***more dis**honest* → ***most dis**honest*

  However, it is more common to say *not as kind as ..., not as honest as ...,* than it is to say *unkinder, more dishonest.*

- When ***than*** is followed by a personal pronoun, it can be a subject pronoun + auxiliary or a subject pronoun + whole clause. In informal English, it is acceptable to use an object pronoun after ***than***:
  *She works harder **than I do**.*
  *She works harder **than me**.* (informal)
  *She works harder **than I used to (work) at her age**.*

- It is not always necessary to follow a comparative with ***than***. A comparative can stand on its own:
  A: *Shall we go by train or by bus?*
  B: *The train's more expensive.*
  A: *Yes, but it's more comfortable.*
  It is clear from the context that the train is being compared with the bus.

- We use ***as*** + adjective + ***as*** to indicate that two things are very similar. And we often use it in the negative: ***not as** ... **as***: *I'm **not as strong as** you are.*

- Two comparatives joined by ***and*** give the idea of a continuing increase:
  *It's growing **bigger and bigger** every day.*
  *It's getting **more and more difficult** to find a quiet beach.*

- We can qualify comparatives using ***a bit, a little, a little bit, quite a bit, a lot, much, far, even, hardly, any, no***:
  *She's **much happier** than she used to be.*
  *He's **even more upset** today than he was yesterday.*
  *Why don't we go on the coach? It's **quite a bit cheaper** than the train.*

Practice

4 Put the adjectives in brackets into the comparative or superlative form. Write the answers for Text 1 under the memo in the spaces provided.

1

Memo

The company's annual report shows that sales figures were [1]..... (low) than the previous year. This is no surprise due to the recession but what is [2]..... (disappointing) than this is the clear evidence that some of our very [3]..... (old) clients have switched to another supplier. We are aware that there are [4]..... (cheap) suppliers than ourselves but this may not be the [5]..... (important) factor. One old client was heard to say that their new supplier was [6]..... (efficient) and [7]..... (flexible) than we are. If this is the case, then this is [8]..... (worrying) than anything else. The economic situation is getting [9]..... and ..... (critical) and if we do not compare favourably with our [10]..... (big) competitors, then we will not survive. We used to have the [11]..... (high) reputation in the business but we are in danger of losing that forever. It is not easy to be the [12]..... (good) but that is what we should be aiming for.

1 *lower* .... 7 ....
2 .... 8 ....
3 .... 9 ....
4 .... 10 ....
5 .... 11 ....
6 .... 12 ....

2 Pam, who lives in London, is on the phone to her friend Debbie, who has recently moved to the countryside.

PAM: So how are you enjoying living in the new place?

DEBBIE: Oh, it's very nice. The house is much [13]................................ (spacious) than the flat we had in London and one of the [14]................................ (good) things is being able to walk out of the back door into our own garden.

PAM: Mm, that must be lovely. So all in all, it's much [15]................................ (good) than London, is it?

DEBBIE: Well, I'm not sure I would say that. It's certainly [16].................................... (polluted) here and I suppose it's [17].................................... (stressful) and that must be good for me. But it's just so much [18].................................... (quiet) here and that takes some time to get used to. I suppose I miss the cultural diversity of London. Going out shopping in London was so much [19].................................... (interesting) than it is here. The people here are so much [20].................................... (varied) than they are in London.

PAM: I suppose that's true. But it's so much [21].................................... (busy) on the streets here in London. It must be nice to walk around somewhere that's much [22].................................... (crowded).

DEBBIE: Well, sometimes it is. Anyway, at least I'm coming up to London next weekend. I'm [23].................................... (excited) about that than I am about anything happening round here.

PAM: Oh dear. You seem to be thinking that you haven't made the [24].................................... (good) decision.

DEBBIE: Well, perhaps I'll feel [25].................................... (settled) here after a few months. Who knows?

PAM: Yes, probably. I personally think you're really lucky to be where you are. When I came to visit you, I thought it was one of the [26].................................... (beautiful) places I'd ever seen.

5 Adverbs and adverbial phrases

Types of adverbs and adverbial phrases

- Adverbs of manner:
  carefully, badly, quickly, in a friendly way:
  *You must pick the glass up very **carefully**.*
- Adverbs of place (location and direction):
  in Cairo, to Egypt, abroad, downstairs, underneath, over here, at my brother's:
  *They're staying **abroad**.*
- Adverbs of time:
  on Saturday, for a long time, now, eventually:
  *I'll see you **on Saturday**.*
- Adverbs of frequency:
  always, often, sometimes, twice a week, monthly, again:
  *I **often** meet him in the park.*
- Adverbs of degree:
  almost, a bit, quite, hardly, very much, only, even:
  *I **quite** like that dress.*
- Sentence adverbs (modifying the whole sentence or clause and often expressing degrees of certainty and/or the speaker's opinion):
  obviously, definitely, presumably, probably, luckily, naturally:
  *The new system is **definitely** an improvement on the old one.*
  ***Hopefully**, I'll be there before 10 o'clock.*

Notes

- Adverbs often add to the meaning of a verb. They tell us *how, when, where,* etc. something was done. However, they do not always modify a verb. They can modify adjectives, nouns, other adverbs, phrases and sentences.
- *When, where, why,* etc. are interrogative adverbs.
- *Very, really,* etc. are adverbs which strengthen adjectives and other adverbs. They are sometimes called intensifiers.
- The second word in a phrasal verb is often an adverb, e.g. *lie **down***.
- Adverbs such as *even, only, just* and *simply* precede the word they qualify and focus attention on it. They are sometimes called focus adverbs.

Position of adverbs

- Adverbs of manner, place and time usually go after an intransitive verb or after a transitive verb + object.

	V ADVERB
Adverbs of manner:	The children sat quietly.
	V O ADVERB
	They did the work quickly.
	V ADVERB
Adverbs of place:	They stayed in a hotel.
	V O ADVERB
	I bought these shoes in the market.
	V ADVERB
Adverbs of time:	They arrived this morning.
	V O ADVERB
	I saw Steve last night.

- Adverbs of manner, place and time can sometimes be placed at the beginning of a sentence for emphasis:
  ***Slowly**, the door started to open.*
  ***In Crete**, we stayed in a beautiful beach villa.*
  ***Last weekend**, I stayed in and did lots of work.*

- It is also possible to place adverbs of manner and adverbs of indefinite time between the subject and the verb:
  *Ben **stupidly** went out without locking the door.*
  *I **recently** changed my job.*
  (NOT ~~*I last month changed my job*~~.)

- If there is more than one kind of adverb in a sentence, the order is usually: manner, place, time:

	Manner	*Place*	*Time*
She waited	*anxiously*	*at the airport*	*for five hours.*

- Adverbs of definite frequency, e.g. ***once, twice, three times a week, daily, every afternoon, on Saturdays, again***, are usually placed at the end of a sentence:
  I go swimming ***twice a week****.*
  I get up at seven o'clock ***every morning****.*
  But they can also go at the beginning of a sentence:
  On Saturdays*, I do my shopping.*

- Adverbs of indefinite frequency, e.g. ***always, usually, sometimes, often, never***, usually go after an auxiliary or the verb *to be* and before a full verb:
  I am ***usually*** *in bed before midnight.*
  I have ***always*** *wanted to go there.*
  We ***sometimes*** *meet for lunch.*

- The adverbs ***frequently, generally, normally, occasionally, ordinarily, sometimes, usually, quite/very often, always/never*** (in the imperative), can also go at the beginning of a sentence for special emphasis:
  Sometimes *he agrees to help me with my homework.*
  Never *do that again!*

- Adverbs of degree, e.g. ***quite, hardly, too,*** usually go before the words they modify:
  quite *nice* ***quite*** *slowly*
  I ***quite*** *enjoyed it.*

- Sentence adverbs, e.g. ***clearly, generally, evidently, honestly,*** can go at the beginning of a sentence:
  Clearly*, the situation is very serious.*
  Or they can go before the verb (or after the verb ***to be*** or an auxiliary):
  I ***honestly*** *believe that this is the best thing we can do.*
  Mr Jameson is ***evidently*** *very happy with the results.*

Practice

5a Write the sentences with the adverbs/adverbial phrases in brackets in the correct position. If the adverbs can go in more than one position, put them in the more usual one.

1 I've been working (in my office/all morning/hard).
I've been working hard in my office all morning.

2 He speaks to me (in the mornings/never/nicely).

....

3 We were listening (all evening/carefully).

....

4 She's been sleeping (in that chair/all afternoon/soundly).

....

....

5 He is (at this time of day/usually/at the college).

....

6 The postman comes (in the morning/very early).

....

7 I thought you spoke (in that meeting/very well/yesterday).

....

....

8 We go swimming (on Saturdays/generally/at the local pool).

....

....

9 I bought these jeans (in the sales/very cheaply/last week).

....

....

10 He's been (to a dentist/never/in his life).

....

5b Complete the story using the following adverbs and adverbial phrases.

for three hours	so much	already	a few times	for months	
lovingly	deeply	just	anxiously	suddenly	soon only
straightaway	hardly	absolutely	~~impatiently~~	in a friendly way	

She waited [1]..*impatiently*.. in the departure lounge. She had [2]...................................... been there [3]...................................... . If she didn't get on the plane [4]...................................... , she might change her mind about going. She had been planning this trip to Berlin [5]...................................... , well, since Uwe had left England. She had missed him [6]...................................... and she could [7]...................................... wait to see him again. But did he love her as [8]...................................... as she loved him? She wasn't [9]...................................... sure. She had written to him every day but he had [10]...................................... written to her [11]...................................... . Would he take her [12]...................................... into his arms as soon as she arrived? Or would he just greet her [13]...................................... ? Oh, how she hated this waiting. [14]...................................... , she heard a message on the tannoy: 'Would Ms Pamela Roberts please go to the desk in the departure lounge [15]...................................... ? A message has [16]...................................... arrived for her.' Pamela walked [17]...................................... towards the desk. What could the message be?

6 Comparison of adverbs

Only gradable adverbs, that is adverbs that can be modified, can have comparative and superlative forms. We cannot modify adverbs such as ***sometimes, never, there, now, almost***.
Adverbs ending in ***-ly*** and a few other adverbs can be put into comparative and superlative forms:

	Adverb	*Comparative*	*Superlative*
*Adverbs ending in **-ly***	carefully quickly	more carefully more quickly	most carefully most quickly
Adverbs with same form as adjective	fast hard early	faster harder earlier	fastest hardest earliest
Irregulars	badly well little much	worse better less more	worst best least most

*She drives **more carefully** than he does.*
*I think Sarah works the **hardest** of us all.*
*He helps me **less** than he used to.*

Notes

- We can also make adverbial comparisons using:
  - (*not*) ***as*** + adverb + ***as***:
    *You walk **as fast as** your brother does.*
    *I can't speak English **as well as** you can.*
  - ***the*** + comparative adverb, ***the*** + comparative adverb or adjective:
    ***The harder** I try, **the worse** I seem to do.*
    ***The more carefully** you do it, **the better** it will be.*
  - comparative adverb + ***and*** + comparative adverb:
    *As the exams got nearer, he worked **harder and harder**.*
    *It's happening **more and more regularly**.*
- superlative adverbs are not used very often.
  We often use comparative + ***than ever, anyone, anything***:
  *You can do the job **better than anyone** can.*

Practice

6a Put the adjectives into the comparative adjective or comparative adverb form.

1 I sleep much ..*more heavily*.. (heavy) than I used to.

2 She's become much ..*happier*.. (happy) since she stopped seeing Dominic.

3 He has to work a lot .... (hard) in this new job than he used to in his old one.

4 I always feel .... (healthy) when I'm on holiday than when I'm at work.

5 It all happened .... (sudden) than I was expecting.

6 I think the meal's going to be a lot .... (expensive) than we anticipated.

7 That child ate .... (hungry) than any child I've ever seen.

8 This curry tastes .... (hot) than you usually make it.

9 I occasionally go to the gym but I should go .... (frequent) than I do.

10 He was injured .... (serious) than any of the others.

11 He made me .... (furious) than I've ever been in my life.

12 He treats her .... (considerate) now than he used to.

13 You need to react .... (assertive) when they treat you like that.

14 The weather's turned .... (cold) recently.

15 Your hair looks much .... (nice) like that.

16 You've upset her now. I think you could have told her .... (tactful).

17 I think you were charged too much. Bill would have done the job .... (cheap) for you.

18 I hope this exam is .... (easy) than the one I did yesterday.

19 She took the news .... (calm) than I thought she would.

6b Put the adjectives and adverbs in brackets into the comparative.
Use: a comparative with ***-er***, a comparative with ***more/less***, a comparative with ***more and more*** or a comparative with ***as ... as***. Write the answers in the spaces provided below the text.

Feel Young and Bright with Suppavite

Are you not [1].... (young) you used to be? Do you feel [2].... and .... (tired) in the mornings? When you get in from work, do you get ready to go out [3].... (quickly) possible so that you can go and meet your friends? No? You probably go out [4].... (often) now than you used to. You just don't seem to have the energy for it anymore. You used to do everything so much [5].... (enthusiastically), but now all you want to do is stay at home.

What you need is Suppavite, an amazing new vitamin supplement that will restore some of that youthful energy. After a couple of weeks of taking Suppavite, you're likely to find that you're getting up [6].... (early), getting things done [7].... fast and approaching life [8].... (energetically) and [9].... (optimistically) than you have done for years. Your friends will wonder how you're coping so much [10].... (well) with the rigours of daily life than they are.

Why don't you try it and see?
You certainly won't regret it.

1 *as young as*..........................

2 ....

3 ....

4 ....

5 ....

6 ....

7 ....

8 ....

9 ....

10 ....

Verbs

7 Simple and continuous aspects

Verbs forms can use either the simple aspect or the continuous aspect.

The infinitive can also be used in the simple or continuous aspect:
*That child is too young **to play** with matches.*
(infinitive with ***to***)
*That child is too young **to be playing** with matches.*
(continuous infinitive with ***to***)

*You shouldn't **work** so hard.*
(modal + infinitive)
*You shouldn't **be working** so hard.*
(modal + continuous infinitive)

The simple aspect

When we use the simple aspect, we view the action or series of actions as a whole.

The simple aspect indicates one or both of the following:

- that an action or series of actions is complete.
- that the situation is permanent or is regarded as permanent.

We can use both dynamic and stative verbs in the simple aspect.

Dynamic verbs are verbs which describe actions, e.g. go, ask, walk, explain, work.

Stative verbs are verbs which do not describe actions: they describe feelings, thoughts, wishes, the senses and states of being, e.g. believe, belong, know, smell, understand, want.

The continuous (or progressive) aspect

When we use the continuous aspect, we view the action or series of actions in progress. The continuous aspect does not describe the whole event.

The continuous aspect indicates one or more of the following:

- that the action or series of actions are in progress. We view the action at some point between its beginning and its end.
- that the action is not complete.
- that the situation is temporary.

When we use the continuous aspect, we describe an activity in progress. We therefore use the continuous aspect with dynamic verbs but not with stative verbs.

Practice

7a Put the verbs in brackets into the tense indicated. Choose between the simple aspect and the continuous aspect.

Jenny and Francesca, two friends, are talking.

J: So what is it that [1]'s worrying. (worry – present) you?

F: Well, I just [2]... (not see – present) a way out of my problems with my boss.

J: Why? What [3]... (go on – present perfect)?

F: Well, we [4].. (go out – past) for dinner about a month ago and I [5]... (think – present) he [6]................................ (assume – past) that I [7].. (be interested – past) in going out with him regularly, but I'm not.

J: [8]... (you/tell – past) him that?

F: Yes, of course I have, but he just [9]... (not seem – present) to understand. Take yesterday for example. I [10]... (work – past) hard on my monthly report when he [11]... (come up – past) to me and [12]... (put – past) his arm round my shoulder. I really [13]................................. (not like – present) him doing that.

J: No, of course. I [14]... (suppose – present) he [15]... (not believe – present) you're not interested in him.

F: No. And he [16]... (get – present) worse all the time. And I [17]... (get – present) more and more fed up with it. In fact I [18]... (think – present) of leaving.

J: But [19]... (you really want – present) to leave?

F: Well no, but I [20]... (not want – present) to be treated like this. Oh well, he's not here today, thank goodness. He [21]... (attend – present) a conference in Birmingham. I [22]... (expect – present) he [23]... (talk – present) to all the attractive women and [24]... (try – present) to find someone to have dinner with.

J: I can tell you really [25]... (dislike – present) him.

Stative and dynamic verbs

- Dynamic Verbs – activities, e.g. drive, watch, listen.
- Stative Verbs – a state of being and not an activity.
  These include:
  feelings – love, hate
  thinking/believing – think, suppose, expect
  wants and preferences – want, need, prefer
  perceptions and the senses – look, smell
  possession – have, own, belong
  being/seeming – be, seem, appear
- Some verbs which are normally stative verbs can become dynamic verbs with some change in meaning:

  *I **hope** to see you this weekend.*
  (expresses a wish)

  *I'**m hoping** to see you this weekend.*
  (Quite a common use. In the continuous form, ***hope*** becomes more of a deliberate action now in progress.)

  *I **think** it's a good idea.*
  (expresses opinion)

  *You're very quiet. What **are** you **thinking** about?*
  (question about the activity of thinking)

  *He'**s** a very foolish person.*
  (description of something about his character)

  *He'**s being** very foolish.*
  (description of how he's acting/behaving at the moment)

  *This wine **tastes** good.*
  (describing the effect on one of the senses)

  *Amy'**s tasting** the wine to see if it's all right.*
  (describing the activity of tasting)

Practice

7b Complete the gaps using the verbs from the box. Each verb is used once as a stative verb and once as a dynamic verb. Put the verbs into the appropriate present simple or present continuous form.

see	think	admire	appear	have
expect	~~weigh~~	look	be	represent

1 How much *do* you *weigh*? About 60 kilos.

2 We .... dinner at the moment so I'll phone you back in half an hour if that's O.K.

3 Harry's been in his room for ages. He .... at all his old photographs.

4 I really .... Helen. She's an excellent manager.

5 Penelope Fitzgerald .... in a new production of Oliver in London's West End.

6 I'm quite happy for your children to come to the party because I know they .... very well-behaved.

7 The snake in this picture .... the forces of evil.

8 They don't really like living here. They .... of moving.

9 .... you .... that man over there with the grey suit on? He's my brother.

10 I'm really looking forward to this holiday. The hotel .... lovely in the photographs.

11 I can't come out tonight because I .... Paul.

12 I'll do it if I can, but I .... not .... much time today.

13 What .... you .... of the management's new proposals?

14 He .... Joan home any minute.

15 'What are you doing in here?'
'I .... just .... this painting. I think it's really beautiful.'

16 'Where's the baby?'
'They .... her. Look, there she is on the scales.'

17 I haven't spoken to him much but he .... to be a very nice man.

18 Look at Nick out in the garden. He .... really nice with the younger children.

19 So Peter's still not here. I .... he's forgotten about the meeting. We should start without him.

20 'I hope you've got a good lawyer.'
'Yes, Alison Medley .... me at the trial. She's the best lawyer in town.

8 The perfect aspect

The use of the perfect aspect indicates that the event took place before the time being referred to **or** that it covered a period of time up to the time being referred to. It also shows that this event has some relevance to the time being referred to:
*John**'s left**.* (present perfect)
John left before the present time.
He is not here now.

*John **had left** when we got there.* (past perfect)
John left before we got there.
He was not there when we got there.

*John **will have left** when we get there.* (future perfect)
John will leave before we get there.
He will not be there when we get there.

The infinitive can also have a perfect aspect:
*He is sure **to be** there.* (infinitive with ***to***)
*He is sure **to have been** there.* (perfect infinitive with ***to***)
(= It is certain that he has been/was there.)

Modals can be followed by the infinitive or the perfect infinitive:
*Pam may **tell** him the news.* (infinitive)
*Pam may **have told** him the news.* (perfect infinitive)
(= It is possible that Pam has told him the news.)

Practice

8 Put the verbs in brackets into the present perfect simple, the past perfect simple or the future perfect simple.

1 The local car factory *has suffered* (suffer) a big drop in sales this year.

2 I .... (work) here for too long. It's time to find a new job.

3 By the time I see my mother tonight, she .... (hear) the news.

4 I was nineteen and studying at university. I .... (be) there for almost a year.

5 It was New Year's Eve but none of the family really wanted to celebrate. They .... (have) a terrible year.

6 They .... (be married) for twenty-five years next month.

7 The doctor came as quickly as she could but the old man .... (already die).

8 She woke up and thought about the night before. It .... (certainly be) a night to remember.

9 Oh no! You look terrible. What .... (happen)?

10 When the ship comes back to port next week, the crew .... (be) at sea for six months.

11 Go and help that child. She .... (fall off) her bike.

12 No one in the village had any money because they .... (all lost) their jobs.

13 By the time the summer comes. I .... (finish) all my exams.

14 There was no one at the meeting. Everyone .... (decide) to boycott it.

15 I hear you're looking for a new job. .... (you/find) one?

THE PRESENT TENSE

9 Present Simple and Present Continuous

Present simple

FORM

I work, etc.
Do/Does + infinitive for questions, negatives and short answers

USE

- A regular repeated activity.
  We often use the present simple in this way with adverbs or adverbial phrases of frequency: *sometimes, never, occasionally, every day, on Saturdays, once a week*, etc:
  I ***catch*** *the 8 o'clock train <u>every day</u>.*
  He ***attends*** *the board meeting <u>every Monday</u>.*

- Something that is generally true; a statement of fact:
  Water ***boils*** *at 100 degrees centigrade.*
  Cats ***don't like*** *water.*
  Where ***do*** *you* ***work****?*

- With stative verbs, that is, verbs that describe sentiments, thoughts and states rather than activities:
  Adrian ***needs*** *your help.*
  That coat ***belongs*** *to me.*

- Instructions:
  (We can use the imperative or the present simple for instructions.)
  You ***take*** *the first turning on the left.*
  You ***mix*** *the soup with some cream at the end.*

- In clauses of time and condition, referring to the future. It is used after: *when, if, unless, before, after, until, as soon as, whenever*, etc:
  I'll give her the message <u>when</u> she ***comes*** *back.*
  Will you tell me <u>if</u> you ***see*** *her?*

- Introducing a quotation:
  This book ***says*** *that too much butter and milk is bad for you.*
  The local newspaper ***says*** *that the government should do more to create jobs in the area.*

- In newspaper headlines:
  RIOTS **BREAK OUT** IN CITY CENTRE
  PRESIDENT **RECEIVES** HUGE WELCOME

- For dramatic narrative.
  It is most often used for dramatic narrative in sports commentating when radio and television commentators describe a short action that is completed as the commentator is speaking:
  And Eastwood ***passes*** *the ball to Andrews.*
  And Miller ***takes*** *the lead in the first lap.*

- To give information about a future event:
  It is used in this way with information about timetables, official events and itineraries:
  *The train **leaves** at 3.30 this afternoon.*
  *The Prime Minister **starts** his official visit to China tomorrow.*
  *You **arrive** at the hotel at about 6.00 and **have** your evening meal at 7.30.*

Present continuous

FORM

Verb **to be** + present participle:
*I **am working**,* etc.

USE

- Activity in progress at this moment:
  *Where'**s** David?*
  *He'**s doing** his homework.*

- An activity that is taking place in the present time period and will continue for a limited time. The activity may or may not be in progress at the moment of speaking.
  The present continuous is often used in this way with *these days, this week, today, this month,* etc:

  *'And what'**s** Linda **doing** these days?'*
  *'She'**s doing** a course in engineering.'*
  (Linda may not be studying engineering at this minute.)

  *The decorator'**s painting** the children's bedrooms this week so they'**re sleeping** in the living room.*
  (The decorators may not be painting at this moment and the children may not be sleeping.)

- A situation that is in the process of changing:
  *Venice **is falling** into the sea.*
  *The number of cars on the road **is increasing** rapidly each year.*

- A future intention with a verb of motion:
  *We'**re driving** up to Scotland next week.*
  *He'**s flying** back on Saturday.*

Practice

9a Put the verbs in brackets into the present simple or present continuous.

1 Debbie ..works.. (work) as an administrator at the university. She .... (organise) all the timetables and teaching schedules. She .... (work) very long hours at the moment because it's the start of the academic year but she .... (go) on a short holiday at the end of the month.

2 Simon and Sylvia .... (stay) in a cottage in the Yorkshire Dales this month. The cottage .... (belong) to a cousin of Sylvia's but the cousin is away: she .... (cycle) around Norfolk for a few weeks. Simon and Sylvia often .... (use) the cottage when Sylvia's cousin is away. They really .... (enjoy) being in the middle of the countryside.

3 The International School for Languages .... (do) very well at the moment. About two hundred students .... (take) evening classes this term. Many of them .... (need) to learn a new language to improve their job prospects but some of them .... (learn) a new language purely for pleasure. The European languages .... (be) very popular but Japanese and Russian .... (get) more popular too. The school .... (provide) good learning facilities and .... (organise) a range of study tours.

4 The world population .... (still increase) rapidly. Many people in the world .... (already starve) and many more .... (suffer) from malnutrition. The population .... (grow) fastest in the poorest countries where people .... (need) to have children to look after them in their old age and where many of their children .... (die) at a very young age.

9b Put the verbs in brackets into the present simple or present continuous.

Maggie and Jill, two friends, are talking at a party.

M: Jill, how nice to see you. I ¹ don't think (not think) we've seen each other since that party at Jim's last year. How ² .... (you/get on)?

J: Oh, fine. Everything ³ .... (go) very well.

M: ⁴ .... (you still/go out) with Dave?

J: No, I'm not, but I ⁵ .... (go out) with someone called Jamie: I met him at my pottery class.

M: Is he here now?

J: Yes look, he's over there. He ⁶ .... (talk) to Charlotte.

M: Oh yes, I ⁷ .... (see) him. ⁸ .... (he/wear) a yellow jumper?

J: Yes, that's him.

M: Oh, he ⁹ .... (look) really nice.

J: He is. I'll introduce you to him when he ¹⁰ .... (come) over here. So what about you? How ¹¹ .... (life/treat) you?

M: Not too badly. I ¹² .... (still/work) at that awful café. I ¹³ .... (keep) looking for other jobs but the problem is that I ¹⁴ .... (feel) so tired when I ¹⁵ .... (get in) that I ¹⁶ .... (not have) much energy to look through all the job ads and everything. Oh well, I ¹⁷ .... (suppose) something else will come up soon.

J: I [18].. (hope) so. Oh look, Jamie
[19].. (come over) here.
[20].. (you/want) to meet him?

M: Oh yes.

THE PAST TENSE

10 Past Simple and Past Continuous

Past simple

FORM

Positive: past simple form of verb: *I* ***arrived***, etc. (regular) *I* ***came***, etc. (irregular) Negative and question form: **did** + infinitive Short answer: **did**

USE

- Completed actions.
  To talk about events and actions in the past that are now finished.
  The past simple refers to the complete event. The time or approximate time that the event took place is stated or is understood from the context. It may be in the very recent past:
  Your mother ***phoned*** *a few minutes ago.*
  Who ***opened*** *this window?*

  or it may be in the more distant past:
  I never ***learnt*** *to swim as a child.*

- Past habit or regular event.
  To talk about a regular, repeated or habitual event:
  We ***went out*** *for a meal every evening on holiday.*
  He ***got up*** *at 7 o'clock every morning to go to work.*

  or a past habit or situation of some duration:
  He ***smoked*** *for most of his life.*
  She ***worked*** *there for twenty years.*

- Past situation at a point in time.
  With stative verbs, to talk about a situation that existed at a certain time in the past:
  In 1950, there ***were*** *fewer than 50 million cars in use around the world.*
  At the time, I ***had*** *a poorly-paid job in the local shop.*

Past continuous

FORM

was/were + present participle: *I **was studying***, etc.

USE

- Used in conjunction with the past simple to describe an action or event that started before the event in the past simple and was in progress when the event in the past simple occurred:
*They **were watching** a film when we arrived.*
*She **was studying** law when the war started.*

- To describe an action, event or situation that was in progress at a specified time in the past:
*In 1982, we **were living** in a small flat in Bristol.*
*In May of last year, she **was studying** hard for her final exams.*
*At 6 o'clock this morning, I **was walking** along the beach.*

- Used with ***while*** to describe two actions that were in progress at the same time:
*While I **was driving** along this morning, I **was thinking** about what you'd said.*
*He **was cooking** the dinner while she **was talking** to him.*

- With adverbials beginning with *all* e.g. ***all night***, ***all morning***, ***all day yesterday***, to show that an action or event was in progress throughout this time:
*I **was watching** television all evening.*
***Were** you **working** all weekend?*

- To describe the background and set the scene for a narrative in the past:
*The wind **was blowing** and the rain **was beating** down. John Snell **was standing** at the bus stop shivering. He **was trying** to imagine being at home sitting by a warm fire. Finally he saw the headlights of the bus approaching from the distance.*

Contrast: past continuous versus past simple

The past simple describes a complete event in the past. The past continuous does not describe the complete event, it describes the event in progress, at some time between its beginning and its end.

Stative verbs, that is verbs that describe thoughts, sentiments and states, cannot normally be put into the continuous form. (See p. 29)

Look at the difference between these sentences:

*He **was cooking** the dinner when I arrived.*
(He started cooking the dinner before my arrival and the cooking was in progress at the time of my arrival.)
*He **cooked** the dinner when I arrived.*
(I arrived and then he cooked the dinner. Two complete events.)

*I **was reading** a book about astrology last night.*
(The reading of the book was in progress last night. The past continuous does not describe the complete event so we assume that the book was not finished last night.)
***I read** a book about astrology last night.*
(I read the whole book from beginning to end last night.)

*It **was raining** all night.*
(The rain was in progress throughout the night. The use of the past continuous emphasizes the continuity and duration of the event.)
*It **rained** all night.*
(It rained from the beginning of the night to the end of the night. The rain is viewed as one single, complete event.)

*While I **was making** the dinner, the children **were watching** television.*
(Two activities in progress at the same time.)
*While I **made** the dinner, the children **watched** television.*
(Two complete events that happened at the same time.)

*I **was having** a bath at 8 o'clock.*
(The bath started before 8 o'clock and was still in progress at 8 o'clock.)
*I **had** a bath at 8 o'clock.*
(This describes the complete event. It started at 8 o'clock.)

Practice

10a Put the verbs in brackets into the past simple or past continuous.

Here he [1].*was*. (be), Davey Stark, the big rock star. It [2]........................... (be) the end of an exhausting two-hour concert. The fans [3]........................... (scream) and [4]........................... (shout). They [5]........................... (want) Davey, their hero. His face [6]........................... (pour) with sweat, his hair [7]........................... (drip) and his heart [8]........................... (thump) violently. But he [9]........................... (love) these moments at the end of a concert. He always [10]........................... (feel) powerful and in control. He [11]........................... (decide) to do one more song for the crowd: one of his most popular. When he

[12]........................... (start) singing, the crowd [13]........................... (go) wild. By the end of the song, they [14]........................... (all/dance) and [15]........................... (clap) their hands. When Davey [16]........................... (leave) the stage, he [17]........................... (be) exhausted but exhilarated. But when he [18]........................... (get back) to the dressing room, he [19]........................... (open) the door and [20]........................... (see) that two men [21]........................... (wait) for him. They [22]........................... (lock) the door behind Davey. He [23]........................... (shout) for his bodyguard Bernard, but no-one [24]........................... (come). The two men [25]........................... (tie) his hands behind his back, [26]........................... (blindfold) and [27]........................... (gag) him. Davey [28]........................... (can hear) Bernard in the next room. Bernard [29]........................... (talk) to someone and he [30]........................... (say) terrible things about Davey. He [31]........................... (say) that Davey [32]........................... (deserve) it. [33]........................... (Deserve) what? What [34]........................... (he/mean)? What [35]........................... (go on)? Why [36]........................... (not someone tell) him what [37]........................... (happen)?

10b Put the verbs in brackets into the past simple or past continuous.

1 It [1] *happened* (happen) in June 1985. It [2]........................... (be) summer and we [3]........................... (all/lie out) in the garden. My mother [4]........................... (read) and my uncle [5]........................... (just/doze) in the sun. We children [6]........................... (look for) worms and insects. And then he [7]........................... (arrive). He [8]........................... (be) a tall, handsome man with piercing blue eyes and he [9]........................... (look) straight at my mother. Her face [10]........................... (go) pale and her eyes [11]........................... (open) wide with shock.
'Arthur, I [12]........................... (think) you [13]........................... (be) dead,' she [14]........................... (say) in a kind of whisper.

2 A: I [15]........................... (phone) you at about 9 o'clock this morning but you [16]........................... (not answer). What [17]........................... (you/do)?
B: Well, I [18]........................... (hear) the phone but I [19]........................... (have) a shower and I [20]........................... (can not) get out in time to answer it. Anyway, what [21]........................... (you/want)?

A: Well, last night I [22]............................ (clear out) that old desk you [23]............................ (give) me when I [24]............................ (come across) a pile of old letters with a red ribbon round them.

B: My letters?

A: Yes, they [25]............................ (be addressed) to you. And they [26]............................ (all/smell) of perfume, a man's perfume.

3 Last night Jake [27]............................ (wake up) at about 3 a.m. As soon as he [28]............................ (wake up), he [29]............................ (listen out) for strange noises but he [30]............................ (not hear) any. His father [31]............................ (snore) in the next room, some central heating pipes [32]............................ (make) a bit of a noise and a tap [33]............................ (drip) in the bathroom. It was all as usual. Jake [34]............................ (open) the window and [35]............................ (look) outside. The moon [36]............................ (be) full and it [37]............................ (shine) brightly. Jake [38]............................ (think) he [39]............................ (see) an owl in one of the trees. He [40]...................... .... (can certainly hear) one. But then he [41]............................ (see) something different. A man – no, it [42]............................ (be) a woman. She [43]............................ (wear) white and she [44]............................ (hide) behind a tree. Suddenly she [45]............................ (run) towards the house.

TENSES WITH THE PERFECT ASPECT

11 Present Perfect Simple and Present Perfect Continuous

Present perfect simple

FORM

have ('ve) / has ('s) + *past participle: I'**ve decided**,* etc.

USE

The present perfect shows a relationship between past time and present time. It can be used in the following ways:

A To describe an action that happened at an indefinite time before the present. For example:

- To refer to things that people have done and experiences they have had. Its connection with the present is that the experience is part of that person in the present:
  *He'**s taught** English in five different countries.*
  ***Have** you **been** round the National Gallery?*
  *I'**ve been** to Spain but I **haven't been** to Italy.*

- When there is very specific evidence in the present of the event that took place in the past:
  *Oh, you'**ve had** a haircut.*
  *I see they'**ve knocked down** the old cinema in the centre of town.*

- Often in news reporting. The use of the present perfect makes the event seem more immediate and of direct relevance to the present:
  *At least twenty people **have been killed** in a motorway crash.*
  *The Prime Minister **has announced** that taxes are to increase from the beginning of next year.*

- After the construction of ***to be*** (in the present) + ordinal or superlative:
  *This is the first time I'**ve been** to London.*
  *She is the most honest person I'**ve** ever **met**.*

B With adverbials.

Used with adverbials that show a connection between the past and the present, e.g. *so far, up to now, lately, already, yet, just*:
*She'**s** already **done** her homework.*
*I'**ve seen** Jane a lot lately.*
*These letters **have** just **arrived**.*

C With a time reference.

Used with reference to a period of time that is still continuing in the present, e.g. *this morning, this afternoon, today, this week, this month, this year, this century*:
*I'**ve read** two books this week.*
*They'**ve been** on holiday twice this year.*

D In clauses of time and condition.
Can be used in clauses of time and condition when, at a certain point in the future, the event will be in the past:
*I'll give you back your ring when I'**ve found** it.*
*I'll go swimming with you on Monday if I'**ve recovered** from this cold.*
*Do you think I could borrow that book after you'**ve finished** reading it?*

E With ***since***, ***for*** and ***how long*** to describe the duration of an activity or situation that started in the past and continues up to the present and possibly into the future:
*She'**s been** away from home for six months.*
*Hello, I **haven't seen** you for ages.*
*He'**s lived** there since he was a child.*
*How long **have** you **had** this problem?*

Present perfect continuous

USE

A To refer to an activity which has been taking place in the recent period up to the present. The activity may have finished shortly before the moment of speaking or finish at the moment of speaking in the present:
*'You look tired. What **have** you **been doing**?'*
*'I'**ve been playing** football.'*

'Have you had a good evening?'
*'Well, I'**ve been watching** this film on television but it's rubbish so I think I'll turn it off now.'*

*They'**ve been going** out a lot recently.*

B With ***since***, ***for*** and ***how long*** to refer to an activity which started in the past and continues up to the present and possibly into the future. Also used with phrases starting with ***all*** (*all day, all night, all morning*), phrases which emphasize the duration of the activity:
*They'**ve been studying** English for three years.*
*John'**s been looking** for a job since he finished university.*
*How long **have** you **been feeling** so depressed?*
*She'**s been working** all day.*

Contrast: present perfect simple versus present perfect continuous

A With no time reference:
*I'**ve been reading** that book.*
(Describes the activity. The book is not finished.)
*I'**ve read** that book.*
(Describes the completion of an event. The book is finished.)

*She'**s been running**.*
(Describes the activity of running.)
*She'**s run** three miles.*
(This describes the completion of the three miles. We cannot say ~~*She's been running three miles*~~.)

*He's **written** a book about wind-surfing.*
(Completed at an unspecified time in the past.)
*He's **been writing** a book about wind-surfing.*
(Describes his recent activity.)

B With a time reference:

We can use both the present perfect simple and the present perfect continuous to describe an activity that started in the past and continues up to the present and possibly into the future:
*They**'ve been studying** English for three years.*
*They**'ve studied** English for three years.*
(Both these sentences are correct. The present perfect continuous puts more emphasis on the continuity of the activity.)

We can use the present perfect simple and the present perfect continuous with ***lately*** and ***recently***:
***I've been working** really hard lately.*
(The activity of working is important.)
***I've done** a lot of work lately.*
(The completion of a lot of work is important.)

Practice

11a Put the verbs in brackets into the present perfect simple or present perfect continuous.

Tim Bryant, a magazine journalist, is interviewing Margaret Rodwell, the founder of a successful company.

TB: So why do you think your company [1] .has been. (be) so successful?

MR: Well, our products [2] .... (fill) a large gap in the market and I think one of the most important things is that we [3] .... (always listen) to our clients and we [4] .... (act) on their comments and suggestions.

TB: And what's a typical day for you?

MR: Well, take today for example. I [5] .... (interview) candidates for a marketing executive post.

TB: And how many [6] .... (you/interview)?

MR: Er, I [7] .... (interview) four so far. And I [8] .... (talk) to clients on the phone on and off all day. I seem to spend a lot of time on the phone. I [9] .... (discuss) some new ideas with them for the transportation and delivery of our products.

TB: Mm, it sounds like a very busy day.

MR: Oh, that's only part of it. I [10].. (have) two meetings, one with Union representatives and one with departmental heads. And I [11].. (also work) on a proposal for a new marketing strategy.

TB: And it's not two o'clock yet!

MR: No, but of course I [12].. (be) here since seven o'clock this morning.

TB: Gosh. And, I hope you don't mind my mentioning this Ms Rodwell, but some rumours [13].. (circulate) about your possible engagement to Mr Grimaldi, the banker.

MR: No, there will be no engagement, though it's true that Mr Grimaldi and I [14].. (see) each other. That's no secret.

TB: When you get the time, I suppose. And is it also true that you [15].. (learn) Russian with a view to introducing your products there?

MR: Yes, I have, but I [16].. (not learn) much yet; there's still a long way for me to go.

11b Put the verbs in brackets into the present perfect simple or present perfect continuous.

1A: You look hot. What [1] *have you been doing*. (you/do)?

B: I [2].. (run).

A: Running! In this heat? How far [3].. (you/run)?

B: About four miles.

2A: What's the problem? You look a bit preoccupied.

B: Yes, I [4].. (think) about Helen.

A: Why? Is there something wrong with her?

B: Well, she [5].. (act) so strangely lately.

A: In what way?

B: Well, some days when she arrives at work, I know that she [6].. (cry). And she [7].. (make) private calls when we're all out at lunch. I just think that something's going on.

A: [8].. (you/talk) to her about it yet?

B: Yes, a few times, and each time she [9].. (say) that there's nothing wrong, but I'm not so sure.

3A: Where [10].. (you/be), Simon?

B: I [11].. (talk) to Mark on the phone. He says he [12].. (try) to phone us all day.

A: Well I [13].. (be) in most of the day but I [14].. (not hear) the phone.

B: That's strange. But anyway, he [15].. (have) a phone call from Jackie's mother and Jackie [16].. (be) in some kind of accident. It's nothing very serious but she's got to stay in hospital overnight.

A: Oh dear. [17].. (she/break) any bones?

B: I'm not quite sure how badly she [18].. (be hurt) but I think we should go and see her tonight.

12 Contrast: present perfect simple versus past simple

*I'**ve been** to Spain and Italy.*
(indefinite time)
*I **went** to Spain a couple of years ago and I **visited** Italy a few times as a child.*
(specific time)

***Have** you **been** busy this morning?*
(It is still the morning now.)
***Were** you busy this morning?*
(This morning is now the finished past.)

***Have** you had a good holiday?*
(You have just returned.)
***Did** you **have** a good holiday?*
(Your holiday finished some time before the question.)

*She'**s starred** in a lot of major films.*
(She is still alive and acting.)
*She **starred** in a lot of major films.*
(Her acting career is finished or she's dead.)

*He'**s been** in the army for fifteen years.*
(And he is still in the army now.)
*He **was** in the army for fifteen years.*
(But he is no longer in the army. The time period of fifteen years finished in the past.)

Practice

12a Put the verbs in brackets into the past simple, present perfect simple or present perfect continuous.

Jake and Michael, two friends, are talking.

J: Hello, I [1] haven't seen (not see) you for ages.

M: No, it must be about two years since we last [2].. (meet). What [3].. (you/do) with yourself?

J: I [4].. (do) all sorts of things. Life [5].. (be) very busy lately. I [6].. (start) a new job at the sailing centre.

M: Really! Doing what?

J: Well, I [7].. (teach) beginners' courses to school groups this term but when those [8].. (finish), I'll be teaching more advanced groups on holiday courses.

M: That sounds great. What about your old job at the tourist office then?

J: Well, I [9].. (work) there for ten years and I quite [10].. (enjoy) the job but I [11].. (want) to do something different. I [12].. (always/enjoy) sailing in my spare time so I [13].. (think) it would be nice to do it for a job.

M: So how long [14].. (you/be) at the sailing centre?

J: For about two months now. I'm sure I [15].. (do) the right thing. It's a really enjoyable job. And what about you?

M: Well, I'm still at the Rembrandt Hotel. I [16].. (work) there for fifteen years now. But I [17].. (have) a promotion so that's good. They [18].. (give) me the job of head receptionist.

J: Oh, that's good news.

M: Yes, it [19].. (make) me feel much better about work. I mean, I [20].. (do) a lot of different jobs at the hotel but I [21]... (never have) a job with this much responsibility before. I [22]... (work) on the reception desk for four years when I [23]... (start) at the hotel – that was before they [24]... (move) me into the office – but I [25]... (be) only a junior receptionist then so I just [26]... (do) what I [27]... (be told) to do.

J: So when [28]... (you/get) the new job?

M: A month ago, after I [29]... (pass) my intermediate exams in Spanish and German at the college. Did you know I [30]... (do) language evening classes at the college for a while now?

J: No, I didn't realize.

M: Yes, I [31]... (decide) that I [32]... (cannot get) any further at work without learning some languages.

J: And so you did! What a good idea.

12b In your notebook, rewrite the following passages putting the verbs into the present perfect simple or past simple.

News [1] *has just come in* (just come in) that there [2]..... (be) an air crash somewhere off the south coast of England. There [3]..... (be) 120 passengers and crew on the plane and it is understood that no survivors [4]..... (be found). Apparently the plane [5]..... (go) mysteriously out of control and [6]..... (plunge) into the sea. Relatives of most of the passengers and crew [7]..... (now be informed) and many of them [8]..... (set off) for the sea rescue base, but they [9]..... (not be given) much hope. Most of the passengers [10]..... (be) on business.

Despite the problems that the government [11]..... (have) in the last two years, it [12]..... (somehow manage) to stay in power. There [13]..... (be) a number of scandals involving government ministers, including one rumour about the Prime Minister himself. It is said that he [14]..... (promise) gifts to certain Members of Parliament in exchange for their vote before he [15]..... (be elected) leader. In spite of all this, the government [16]..... (maintain) its position in Parliament and [17]..... (claim) that this [18]..... (be) the most successful term of office that a government [19]..... (ever have). This is rather surprising as they [20]..... (come) to power with only a small majority.

13 Past Perfect Simple

The past perfect simple is used to refer to a past time which preceded the past time already being referred to.
It is used in combination with other past tenses to clarify the sequence of events in a past narrative.

FORM

had ('d) + *past participle: I* ***had finished***, etc.

USE

- In sentences which have a ***when*** + past simple clause.
  It is used to make it clear that the event in the past perfect came before the event in the past simple:
  When I got to the station, the train ***had left***.
  (The train left before I got to the station.)

  Compare with:
  When I got to the station, the train left.
  (The train left as I arrived or immediately after my arrival.)

- In ***when*** clauses.
  It is used when we need to make it clear that the event in the **when** clause was completed before the event in the past simple started:
  When I ***had read*** *the letter, I started to cry.*
  (I finished the letter before I started to cry.)

  Compare with:
  When I read the letter, I started to cry.
  (I started to cry after I started reading the letter.)

  We can also use the past perfect in this way with ***as soon as, the moment, immediately***:
  As soon as I ***had told*** *her the news, I regretted it.*

Note: As the action in a ***when*** + past simple clause happens just before the other past simple clause, it is not generally necessary to use the past perfect in the ***when*** clause. We only do this when we need to make it clear that the event in the ***when*** clause was completed before the event in the past simple clause started.

- In ***after*** clauses:
  After we ***had passed*** *our exams, we went out to celebrate.*

  We can also say:
  After we passed our exams, we went out to celebrate.

  The use of the past perfect merely emphasizes the fact that the event in the ***after*** clause preceded the other event. It is correct to use either the past perfect or the past simple in ***after*** clauses.

- As the equivalent of the present perfect.
  The present perfect looks back from the past:
  Ann and Michael have just got married.
  It was June 1991. Ann and Michael ***had just got married***.
  Jeremy's 21 now and he's been in a wheelchair since he was 10.
  Jeremy was 21 and he ***had been*** *in a wheelchair since he was 10.*
  (Note that we use ***was*** in the *since* clause in both sentences.)

- As the equivalent of the past simple. We use it when we want to narrate events looking back from a point in the past. Unlike the present perfect, the past perfect can be used with a specific time reference:

  Jane MacDonald is now 28. She started working for the company when she was eighteen. She quickly climbed the career ladder and is now the youngest managing director the company has ever appointed.

  *Jane MacDonald was then 28. She **had started** working for the company when she was eighteen. She **had** quickly **climbed** the career ladder and is now the youngest managing director the company has ever appointed.*

Notes

- The verb in the *when* clause remains in the past simple when the main verb is in the past perfect: *She had started working for the company when she **was** eighteen.*
- For reasons of style, the narration is not likely to continue for very long in the past perfect. The story usually returns quite quickly to the main time reference point, which is in the past simple.
- If we narrate the events in the order in which they occurred, there is no need for the past perfect: *Jane MacDonald started working for the company when she **was** eighteen. She quickly **climbed** the career ladder and **became** the youngest ever managing director at the age of 28.*

- In reported speech:
  A statement or question in the present perfect is usually put into the past perfect in reported speech:
  I've had a lovely time.
  *She said she **had had** a lovely time.*

  A statement or question in the past simple can be put into the past perfect or remain in the past simple in reported speech:
  I tried to phone you earlier.
  *He said that he **had tried** to phone me earlier.*
  or *He said that he tried to phone me earlier.*

- After *if, wish, if only:*
  *If I **had known** you were at home, I would have called you.*
  *I expect you wish you **had** never **met** him.*
  *If only they **had stayed** at home.*

Practice

13a Put the verbs in brackets into the past simple or past perfect simple.

1 A: I'm sorry we're late. We [1]..missed.. (miss) the train.

B: How [2]............................ (that/happen)?

A: Well, I [3]............................ (get) the times wrong and when we [4]............................ (arrive) at the station, the train [5]............................ (just leave).

2 A: [6]........................... (you/have) a good meal at Hilary's?

B: Well no, it [7]........................... (be) very embarrassing. When we [8]........................... (arrive), we [9]........................... (know) immediately that she [10]........................... (forget) about the whole thing.

A: So what [11]........................... (she/do)?

B: Well, she [12]........................... (pretend) that she [13]........................... (not forget) and [14]........................... (say) that the meal [15]........................... (not be) ready because she [16]........................... (get) home from work very late.

A: Oh no, how awful!

3 It [17]........................... (be) a beautiful morning. It [18]........................... (rain) in the night and so the ground [19]........................... (be) fresh and clean and it [20]........................... (smell) wonderful. None of the Taylor family [21]........................... (be) awake though. They [22]........................... (all go) to bed very late the night before. Their Australian cousin [23]........................... (arrive) unexpectedly that evening and they [24]........................... (sit up) talking most of the night. Although it [25]........................... (be) now 8 o'clock in the morning, they [26]........................... (only be) in bed for about two hours.

13b Put the verbs in brackets into the past simple or past perfect simple.

James [1]..*sat*. (sit) outside the office waiting for the interview. He [2]........................... (feel) so nervous that he [3]........................... (not know) what to do with himself. The person who [4]........................... (go in) before him [5]........................... (be) in there for nearly an hour. And she [6]........................... (look) so confident when she [7]........................... (go in). Not like James. He [8]........................... (feel) sure that she [9]........................... (already get) the job. The problem [10]........................... (be) that he [11]........................... (want) this job so much. It [12]........................... (mean) everything to him. He [13]........................... (think) about it such a lot before the day of the interview. He [14]........................... (imagine) himself performing brilliantly at the interview and being offered the job immediately. But now here he [15]........................... (be) feeling terrible. He [16]..................................... (cannot remember) all those things he [17]........................... (plan) to say. At that moment, he [18]...........................

(almost decide) to get up and leave. But no – he [19]............................ (have to do) this. He [20]............................ (spend) so much time thinking about it that he [21]................................... (cannot give up) like that. His hands [22]............................ (be) hot and sticky and his mouth [23]............................ (feel) dry. Finally the door of the office [24]............................ (open). The woman who [25]............................ (go in) an hour earlier [26]............................ (come out) looking very pleased with herself. She [27]............................ (smile) sympathetically at James. At that moment James [28]............................ (hate) her. The managing director then [29]............................ (appear) at the office door. 'Would you like to come in now, Mr Davis? I'm sorry to have kept you waiting.' James [30]............................ (suddenly wish) that he [31]............................ (go) home after all. He [32]............................ (get up), legs shaking and forehead sweating and [33]............................ (wonder) whether he [34]............................ (look) as terrified as he [35]............................ (feel).

14 Past Perfect Continuous

FORM

had ('d) been + *present participle: I **had been** running,* etc.

USE

The past perfect continuous is the equivalent of the present perfect continuous. The present perfect continuous describes an activity looking back from the present and the past perfect continuous describes an activity looking back from the past:
I'm very tired. I've been working all day.
*I was very tired. I **had been working** all day.*

Why are you so wet? What have you been doing?
*Why were you so wet? What **had** you **been doing**?*

The dog from next door has been barking for two hours.
*It was 1 o'clock and the dog from next door **had been barking** for two hours.*

'It's been raining here for days,' she said.
*She said it **had been raining** there for days.*
(Present perfect continuous becomes past perfect continuous in reported speech.)

Practice

14 In your notebook, rewrite the following passage, making all the necessary tense changes.

It's 10 o'clock at night. The offices of 'The Daily News' are buzzing with excitement. The deadline for the paper is in half an hour and they are frantically trying to finish the front page. Everyone has been working all evening without a break. Some of the journalists have been at the office since early morning. They have all been trying to get an exclusive story, to find out something that no other journalist has discovered. The main story is a big one. The Prime Minister has resigned. Everyone knows that his government has had lots of problems in the last year but his resignation is nonetheless a big surprise. Rumours have been going round all day about the real reasons for the announcement. Some say that he has been involved in some financial scandal. Others say that he has been seeing another woman. All the papers have been working all day to get the best story. And they've been doing their best to find out what the other papers have said. The whole day has been very tense. Suddenly the editor asks everyone to be quiet. There is a telephone call from the Prime Minister's office.

Example: *It was 10 o'clock at night. The offices of 'The Daily News' were buzzing with excitement.*

FUTURE FORMS

15 The *be going to* future and the Present Continuous as future

The *be going to* future

We can express the future with ***be going*** + ***to***–infinitive. This is often referred to as the ***going to*** or ***be going to*** future.

FORM

verb **to be** + **going** + *to*–infinitive: ***I'm going to stay***, etc.

USE

- To express intention. The speaker had the intention before the time of speaking:
  I'm going to visit *Bob tomorrow.*
- To make a prediction based on present evidence:
  *The sun's going down. It**'s going to be** dark in half an hour.*

Present continuous as future

We can use the present continuous to refer to the future. A future time reference must be stated or be clear from the context.

USE

- To describe arrangements. We use it to talk about the future when the plans have been made. It is quite informal and is used to describe personal arrangements such as social activities rather than official plans. As it refers to personal arrangements, the subject of the verb should be a person or people and not a thing:
  I'm meeting *Charlotte for lunch tomorrow.*

Contrast: *be going to* future versus present continuous as future

- a) ***I'm going to visit*** *my aunt in hospital tomorrow.*
  b) ***I'm visiting*** *my aunt in hospital tomorrow.*

  Both these sentences are correct and the difference between them is slight. Sentence a) places more emphasis on the **intention** and sentence b) places more emphasis on the **arrangement**.
  We do not generally use the present continuous with activities that do not involve the making of an arrangement or plan. We can say: *'I'm going to write a letter to my parents tonight.'* (the intention is important) but we do not say: *'I'm writing a letter to my parents tonight.'* (no arrangement is required).

  We tend to avoid using verbs of motion, e.g. ***to go*** and ***to come*** in the ***be going to*** future and prefer instead to use the present continuous with these verbs:
  We're going *to the theatre tonight.*

- a) *Look at that helicopter coming down. It**'s going to land** in a minute.*
  b) *Look at that helicopter coming down.* ~~*It's* ***landing*** *in a minute*~~.

  Sentence a) is correct but sentence b) is not possible. We do not use the present continuous to make a prediction based on present evidence.

- We can only use the present continuous as future with a future time reference or where the future time reference is clear from the context. Where this is not the case, we use the ***be going to*** future:
  *He**'s having** a swim.* (= now, if there is no time reference)
  *He**'s going to have** a swim.* (in the future)

- Verbs not normally used in the continuous are not used in the present continuous as future. We cannot say: ~~***I'm needing*** *some help next week*~~.
  We can sometimes use verbs not normally used in the continuous with the ***be going to*** future. This does not happen very often as these verbs do not describe events that we normally predict or intend. We can say:
  I'm going to need *some help next week.*

Practice

15 In your notebook, rewrite the dialogue, substituting the verbs in the ***be going to*** future with the present continuous as future where this is possible.

A: [1]Are you going to come to the meeting tomorrow about the proposed staff cuts?
B: Oh yes, definitely.
A: Have you read the report about the cuts?
B: No, not yet. [2]I'm going to read it tonight. What does it say?
A: Well, [3]there are going to be quite a few cuts in this department.
B: Oh no. I wonder [4]who's going to lose their job.
A: I don't know. I think [5]they're going to ask people if they want to take voluntary redundancy.
B: Well, I certainly don't want that. [6]We're going to move into a new flat next month and the rent's quite high. I don't know [7]what's going to happen if I lose my job.
A: Oh, don't worry about it too much. I'm sure [8]everything's going to be all right. Look, why don't we go out for drink after work.
B: I can't. [9]I'm going to meet some friends for a meal and then [10]we're going to go to the cinema.
A: Well what about tomorrow night? [11]Are you going to go out then?
B: No, [12]I'm not going to do anything.
A: So let's go out after the meeting.
B: OK. Good idea.

Example:
1 Are you coming ...

16 Future with *will*

This is also referred to as the future simple or simple future tense.

FORM

will ('ll) + *bare infinitive: I* ***will (I'll) go,*** etc. Short form of **will not: won't**

USE

- To make a statement of fact or a prediction about the future:
  Sam ***will be*** *here tomorrow.*
  Tonight's programme ***will be*** *very interesting.*
- To make formal announcements of future plans and to present weather forecasts. It is therefore often used in newspapers and on the television and radio:
  The new President ***will move*** *into the White House tomorrow.*
  Rain ***will continue*** *throughout the day.*
- To express hopes, expectations, thoughts about the future. Used after verbs like: *assume, believe, doubt, expect, hope, reckon, suppose, think* and *be sure/ afraid* and with adverbs like *perhaps, possibly, probably, definitely*:
  *I expect they**'ll be** here soon.*
  *Do you think she**'ll bring** her boyfriend?*
- In sentences containing clauses of condition or time:
  *If I get that job, I**'ll go** out and celebrate.*
  *I**'ll phone** you when I get there.*
- To express an intention when the decision is made at the time of speaking:
  A: *There isn't any milk left.*
  B: *Oh, isn't there? I**'ll get** some in town. I'm going there later on.*
- To express the idea of willingness:
  *I**'ll do** it for you, I promise.* (promise)
  Will *you* ***open*** *the window, please?* (request)
  *I**'ll look after** the children for you.* (offer)
  He ***won't come*** *with me.* (refusal)
  *Yes, I**'ll come** with you.* (agreement)
  I'll definitely ***tell*** *him the truth this time.* (determination)
  *Stop that or I**'ll call** the police.* (threat)
- To make offers or suggestions or to ask for suggestions, advice, instructions. Use ***Shall I/we*** ... in the question form:
  Shall *I* ***help*** *you with that?* (offer)
  Shall *we* ***invite*** *them round for dinner?* (suggestion)
  What ***shall*** *I* ***do****?*
  Shall *we* ***come*** *round after dinner?*

Notes
The use of ***shall***

- In spoken English, **shall** is most often used in the question form with ***I*** or ***we*** to make offers or suggestions or to ask for suggestions, advice, instructions:
  Shall *I come with you?*
  What ***shall*** *we do tomorrow?*

- ***Shall*** is occasionally used to express strong determination about oneself or someone else:
  I ***shall*** *go anyway. I don't care what you think.*
  I ***shan't*** *let him bully me.*
  You ***shall*** *have whatever you want.*

- ***Shall*** can be used in the same way as ***will*** in the first person but ***will*** is more common. In spoken English, the contraction ***'ll*** is the most common.
  Shall is used more frequently in formal written English than in informal written or spoken English:
  We ***shall*** *make every effort to answer your enquiry as soon as possible.*
  I ***shall*** *be at the airport to meet you in person.*

- Short form of ***shall not***: ***shan't.***

Practice

16 Complete the following sentences with ***will/'ll*** or ***shall/'ll*** and a verb from the box.

offer	make	tell	have	~~buy~~	drop	wash	announce
receive	be sentenced	phone	carry	be	invite	go	

1 I'm sorry about losing that book. I.'ll buy.. you another one next week.
2 I .... one of those cases for you.
3 The temperature .... significantly during the afternoon.
4 .... you .... me when you get the news? You've got my number haven't you?
5 The Chancellor .... the details of the budget at 10 o'clock tomorrow.
6 .... we .... her the truth about what happened?
7 I expect they .... here soon.
8 You .... your exam results by post during the first few days of August.
9 I .... not .... them here again, whatever you say.

10 If he is found guilty, he .... to life imprisonment.

11 I .... never .... the same mistake again.

12 .... we .... for a swim this afternoon?

13 They definitely .... not .... me the job: I had a terrible interview.

14 .... I .... these plates?

15 I'm determined that he .... everything he wants.

17 Contrast: *be going to* versus *will*

Intention

The ***be going to*** and ***will*** futures can both be used to express an intention about the future.

- ***be going to:*** the intention is premeditated. The decision was made before the time of speaking or writing and plans have probably already been made:
  A: *You know it's Emily's birthday on Friday, don't you?*
  B: *Yes, I'**m going to buy** her a present this afternoon.*
- ***will:*** the intention is unpremeditated. The decision is made at the time of speaking or writing:
  A: *You know it's Emily's birthday on Friday, don't you?*
  B: *Actually I'd forgotten. Thanks for reminding me. I'**ll buy** her a present this afternoon.*

Prediction

The ***be going to*** and ***will*** futures can both be used to make predictions about the future.

- ***be going to:*** the prediction is based on some form of evidence that exists in the present.
  It is often used to predict what is about to happen but it can be used to predict something that is not in the immediate future:
  *Oh look! That car **is going to crash**.*
  *That child eats too much. He'**s going to be** really overweight one day.*
- ***will:*** to express beliefs, hopes, thoughts, assumptions and doubts about the future:
  *It'**ll be** a difficult year for the new Prime Minister.*
  *I'm sure you'**ll enjoy** yourself there.*

Statement of future fact

The ***be going to*** and ***will*** futures can both be used to make statements about the future but the emphasis is slightly different:
a) *The number of students* ***will fall*** *over the next five years.*
b) *The number of students* ***is going to fall*** *over the next five years.*

Sentence a) is a statement of future fact or of the speaker's beliefs.
Sentence b) is also a statement of future fact but it emphasizes that the speaker is thinking of present trends. It makes the speaker seem more involved and is thus more informal.

Expression of willingness

Will is often used to express willingness.
Be going to does not have this meaning:
I'll ***help*** *you as much as I can.*
(expression of willingness: a promise)
I'm going to help *you as much as I can.*
(expression of intent)

Summary

- ***Be going to*** always indicates a link with the present.
  a) present intention/plans/preparations
  b) present evidence of a future event
- When we use ***will***, the emphasis is more on the future than on its link with the present.
- ***Will*** is more formal than ***be going to*** and is therefore used more extensively in written English.

Practice

17 Put the verbs into the ***be going to*** future or the ***shall/will*** future. If both tenses are possible, choose the one that is most appropriate for the context. With the verbs *to go* or *to come* use the present continuous as future instead of the ***be going to*** future.

Two friends, Jack and David, are talking.

J: Have you decided what you [1]*are going to do* (do) this weekend?

D: Yes, we [2].. (have) a quiet day on Saturday and then on Sunday we [3].. (take) a bus up into the mountains and do some walking. And we [4]...................................... (probably book into) a hotel there for the night. What about you? [5].. (you/do) lots of work as usual?

J: Well, no. Mark phoned last night about coming down this weekend.

D: Really?

J: Yes, he [6].. (come) on Friday.

D: Oh, I'd like to see him. I think I [7].. (phone him up) tonight and arrange something.

J: Well, we're planning to spend the day on the beach on Saturday. We [8].. (do) some swimming and sunbathing. I just hope the weather [9].. (be) warm enough. And then on Saturday night we [10].. (see) that new film with Tom Cruise.

D: Well, as I've got nothing planned, I [11].. (join) you at the beach on Saturday then, if that's O.K.

J: Of course it is. I [12].. (pick you up) from your flat some time after breakfast.

D: Oh thanks. [13].. (I/bring) a picnic?

J: Yes. Why not? I tell you what: Mark and I [14].. (make) some sandwiches and [15].. (you/bring) some salad and fruit?

D: Yes, fine. I [16].. (do) that. Good. That [17].. (save) us all the cost of eating out. And what about the film? What time [18].. (you/see) that?

J: We [19].. (see) the early showing at 6.00 and then we [20].. (try out) that new disco in town.

D: Right. Well, I think I [21].. (spend) the evening at home with Sarah.

J: O.K. So I [22].. (see) you on Saturday morning, probably at around 10 o'clock.

D: Fine.

18 Present Simple as future

USE

- We use the present simple to refer to the future in clauses of time and condition, e.g. after *if, unless, when, as soon as, until, before, after, by the time*:
  *We'll phone you when we **get** there.*
  *Please wait here until I **get** back.*

  And after *everything, anything, whatever, It is important,* etc:
  *Everything that you **say** will be recorded.*
  *You will do whatever I **ask** you to.*

- We can use the present simple to refer to future events when the event is part of a fixed timetable, e.g. a travel timetable, a holiday itinerary, other organized events, an official trip by a member of the government. The event or the timing of the event is fixed by some official body, organization or timetable:
  *The flight **leaves** at 6 o'clock in the morning.*
  *You **spend** the first night of the trip in a hotel in London.*

Practice

18 Where possible, put the verbs in brackets into the present simple. Where this is not possible, use the ***will*** future.

A teacher is giving some students the details of a forthcoming trip.

The coach 1 ...leaves... (leave) here at 9.00 a.m., and we 2 .... (arrive) at the field study centre before lunch. When we 3 .... (get) there, you 4 .... (be shown) to your rooms and 5 .... (be given) time to unpack. Lunch 6 .... (be served) in the dining-room at 12.30 precisely so make sure you 7 .... (not get) there late. When lunch 8 .... (finish), it 9 .... (be) time to get ready for our first activity: a walk down to the beach to look at the rock pools.

Nets, magnifying glasses and containers [10]................................... (be provided) by the centre. It the weather [11]................................... (be) fine, we [12]................................... (stay) on the beach for the whole of the afternoon. Otherwise, we [13]................................... (go back) to the centre after an hour or two and watch a video on seashore life. You [14]................................... (be expected) to keep a written record of everything that you [15]................................... (find) and we [16]................................... (look) at all the records when we [17]................................... (get back) to school at the end of the week. Mr McNeill, the field study supervisor, is very knowledgeable and I'm sure that he [18]................................... (help) you to identify anything that you [19]................................... (not recognize). Supper [20]................................... (be served) at 6.00, and at 8.00 there [21]................................... (be) an evening activity. On the first night, Mr McNeill [22]................................... (plan) to go on a moonlight walk with us to look for bats. It is important that you [23]..................... (stay) together on this walk. Please don't wander off. It [24]................................... (not be) easy for us to find you if you [25]................................... (get lost) in the dark. Behave sensibly and I'm sure you [26]................................... (all have) a wonderful time.

19 Future Continuous

FORM

will be + present participle: ***I'll be coming***, etc.

USE

- To describe an activity that will be in progress at a point in the future:
  *This time tomorrow we'**ll be sitting** on the plane.*
- To describe an activity that will cover the whole of a future time period:
  ***I'll be working** in the office all evening.*
- To describe a future event without expressing deliberate intention:
  Sue: *Oh dear, I haven't given Ben that book back.*
  Joe: *That's all right. I'**ll be seeing** him at the music club tonight so I'll give it to him for you.*

  Here, the activity of seeing Ben is not an express intention but will happen when Joe goes to the music club.

  *I'**ll be revising** for my exams this weekend so I think I'll stay in on Saturday night.*
  The intention expressed here is to stay in on Saturday night. The plan to revise is relevant to this decision.

- To describe what we assume someone else is doing at this moment:
  *Don't phone her now. It's 4 o'clock and she'**ll be collecting** the children from school.*

Note: The future continuous is not used with verbs that do not normally take the continuous form. See page 27.

Contrast: future continuous versus *will* future

will future: expresses intention, belief, hope, assumption and willingness
future continuous: indicates future activity or event but does not express intention or willingness

I'**ll come** and visit you tomorrow	*intention / promise*
I'**ll be coming** to visit you tomorrow so I can bring the magazines then.	*future activity in normal course of events*
Will you **come** to the meeting tonight?	*request*
Will you **be coming** to the meeting tonight?	*casual question about future event*

Practice

19 Put the verbs in brackets into the ***will*** future or the future continuous. Complete any short answers with ***will*** or ***won't***.

1 A: Would you like to come over for lunch on Saturday?
B: Well unfortunately, I [1] *'ll be working* (work) all day Saturday.
A: Oh, that's a shame. Well, you [2] .... (have to come over) another day. I [3] .... (talk) to Andy about it and I [4] .... (phone) you on Sunday. [5] .... (you/be) in then?
B: Yes definitely. I [6] .... (recover) from my week's work.

2 A: [7] .... (you/go) to the meeting tonight? If so, I [8] .... (give) you a lift there.
B: Oh yes please, that would be helpful. I [9] .... (play) tennis until 7 o'clock but I [10] .... (be) back shortly after that.

A: O.K. I [11].. (pick you up) at about 7.30.

[12].. (you/be) ready by then?

B: Yes. Don't worry. I [13].. (wait) for you when you get here.

3 A: Do you ever think about what you [14].. (do) in ten years' time?

B: Oh yes. I sometimes imagine that I [15].. (do) a very important job and earning lots of money and that I [16].. (live) in a beautiful big house. But to be honest, I think I [17].. (still work) here and I [18].. (probably do) the same job.

A: No, you [19].. . You [20].. (get) a better job soon, I'm sure you [21].. .

B: And so [22].. you.

A: And then we [23].. (go) on wonderful foreign holidays and we [24].. (learn) to speak different languages.

B: Perhaps.

4 A: Oh dear, I've run out of stamps. I [25].. (not be able to post) these letters now.

B: Well, I [26].. (go) to the post office later on. I [27].. (take) the letters and post them for you.

A: Oh thank you. I [28].. (give) you the money for the stamps.

5 A: So I [29].. (wait) for you when you get to the station. I [30].. (not come) onto the platform but I [31].. (see) you by the ticket office.

B: O.K., that's fine. I [32].. (carry) a heavy suitcase so I think we [33].. (have to get) a taxi from the station.

20 Contrast: future continuous versus present continuous as future

Present continuous as future: used for plans. The intention is not important.
Future continuous: can also be used to refer to plans. It is not generally used when we first tell someone about a plan. It is often used to refer to a plan when this plan is relevant to the main future event in the sentence:
*We**'re spending** the summer on the coast.* (Telling someone about our plans)
A: *Have you ever been sailing?*
B: *No, but we**'ll be spending** the summer on the coast so I might try it then.*
(Referring to the arrangement to spend summer on the coast in connection with the main idea of the sentence – to try sailing)

A: ***Will** you **be using** your bike tomorrow?*
B: *No, I won't.*
A: *Well, I wonder if I could borrow it for the afternoon.*
(Asking about plans in order to make a request for the future that is connected to those plans)

Practice

20 Put the verbs in brackets into the present continuous or the future continuous. It is often the case that either tense is correct. Choose the tense that you think is the most appropriate.

1 A: *Will you be seeing* (you/see) Tony at work tomorrow?

B: Yes, I *will* .

A: Do you think you could give him a message for me?

2 A: Where .... (you/go) this summer?

B: We .... (go) to the Pyrenees for a couple of weeks in July to do some walking.

3 A: Have you read the notes for the meeting?

B: No, not yet, but I .... (sit) on the train for three hours tomorrow so I can do it then.

4 A: Can you post this letter for me on your way to work?

B: I'm sorry but I .... (not walk) past the post box this morning because Emma .... (give) me a lift to work. I'll post it for you later on though.

5 A: What .... (you/do) tonight? .... (you/go round) to Rita's with us?

B: No, I don't think so. I .... (see) quite a lot of her at our play rehearsals next week.

6 A: I must collect my new glasses from the optician.

B: Do you want me to collect them? I .... (go) past there later on anyway.

21 Future Perfect Simple and Continuous

To talk about the past from a point in the future. It is the equivalent of the present perfect with the reference point in the future. The present perfect looks back from now: the future perfect looks back from the future.

FORM

Future perfect simple:	**will have** + *past participle:*
	I'll have finished, etc.
Future perfect continuous:	**will have been** + *present participle:*
	I'll have been working, etc.

USE

- We use the future perfect simple to say that, at a certain time in the future, something will be completed and be in the past. It is often used with ***by*** + time reference:
  I'll have finished *this book by tomorrow.*
  I'll have told *him the news by the time you get here.*
- We use the future perfect simple and continuous with ***for*** to talk about the duration of an activity or state up to a time in the future:
  *We'**ll have lived** here for two years in January.*
  *She'**ll have been working** here for ten years soon.*
- We use the future perfect continuous to describe an activity leading up to a time in the future:
  *They might be tired when you see them because they'**ll have been working** hard.*

Practice

21 Put the verbs in brackets into the present simple, future simple, future perfect simple or future perfect continuous.

1 I think she *will have heard* (hear) all about it by the time I *see* (see) her.

2 I reckon I .... (finish) this book by the weekend and then I .... (give) it to you.

3 The children .... (be) hungry when they .... (get in) because they .... (run around) all afternoon.

4 This government .... (be) in power for eight years soon but I don't think they .... (win) the next election.

5 .... (you/eat) when you .... (get) here? If not, I .... (make) you something.

6 Don't phone them now. They .... (not get) home yet. They .... (probably get back) at about half-past eight.

7 I think they .... (finish) building the house by the time the winter .... (come) and then we .... (move in) in the New Year.

8 I expect they .... (be) tired when you .... (see) them because they .... (work) all day.

9 If I .... (come) and see the film with you on Saturday, I .... (see) it six times. But it is my favourite film of all time: I think you .... (love) it.

10 Why don't you come round at 9 o'clock? The children .... (go) to bed then so it .... (be) nice and peaceful.

22 Other ways of referring to the future

As well as all the forms we use to refer to the future, we can also use a range of verbs and expressions to show that we are talking about the future. These verbs and expressions are often more precise than a future form and they are used widely, particularly in written English.

- BE TO (***am/is/are/was/were*** + ***to***-infinitive)
  Used for formal plans, official arrangements, instructions and prohibitions:
  The British Ambassador ***is to meet*** *the President at the White House on Friday.*
  The factory ***is to close*** *for three weeks for repairs.*
  She ***is to become*** *the youngest Member of Parliament in our history.*
  *You****'re to be*** *there by eight o'clock.*
  *You****'re not to cross*** *the road without me.*

- BE DUE TO / ABOUT TO / ON THE POINT OF
  be due + ***to***-infinitive: used for arrangements that are to take place at a fixed time. Often used with timetables and official itineraries:
  *The plane****'s due to arrive*** *in half an hour.*
  *Clare****'s due to have*** *her operation in three weeks' time.*

  be (just) about + ***to***-infinitive: used to refer to something that will happen very soon, in the immediate future:
  *Don't start talking to them now: they****'re about to leave****.*

  be (just) on the point of + gerund or noun: used to refer to something in the very immediate future:
  It is understood that the Chancellor ***is on the point of announcing*** *his resignation.*

- CERTAIN VERBS + *TO*-INFINITIVE
  We can say:
  They ***are going to build*** *a new shopping centre in town.*
  We can also use a verb that refers to the future and say:

They	**plan** **intend** **are proposing** **hope** **have agreed** **have promised**	**to build** a new shopping centre in town.

Note: that ***intend*** and ***propose*** can also be followed by a gerund:
They ***intend/propose building*** *a new shopping centre in town.*

We often use a verb that refers to the future, instead of a future form, particularly in written English.

Practice

22 Rewrite the sentences using ***be (not) to, due to, about to, on the point of, plan/intend/propose/hope/agree/promise (not) to.***
You may use a verb or expression more than once.

1 I'm sorry I can't talk to you now. I'm going to work in a minute.
I'm sorry I can't talk to you now. I'm about to go to work.

2 The Council have decided what they would like to do one day. They are going to close the old swimming pool.
The Council intend to close the old swimming pool.

3 They are making plans now. They are going to have a big wedding in the summer.

....

4 The train will depart at 8.25.

....

5 The Condor Freight Company have had discussions with staff representatives and they have reached an agreement on work clothes. They are going to provide free work clothes to all employees.

....

....

6 You must not enter the building without signing your name in the register.

....

....

7 The Government have made a promise. They will not increase taxes during the next year.

....

....

8 The economy will collapse in the very near future; it will happen at any time now.

....

....

9 The Department of Social Security has made a proposal. It is probably going to cut unemployment benefit.

....

....

10 My grandfather is going to die soon.

....

11 I hope I'll find a new job before the end of the year.

....

12 Do you promise that you won't tell anyone about this?

....

13 What are the two leaders' intentions? When are they going to meet?

....

14 They are making plans. They are going to move abroad.

....

15 You will arrive at the hotel at 7.30 in the evening.

....

THE PASSIVE

23 Forms and uses of the passive

FORM

To be in the appropriate form + *past participle.*

- The passive is not used in the present perfect continuous, the past perfect continuous or the future continuous for reasons of style.
- We can use the passive in all other tenses and in other verb forms.

	Active	*Passive*
Infinitive	to do	to be done
Perfect Infinitive	to have done	to have been done
Participle and Gerund	doing	being done
Perfect Participle/Gerund	having done	having been done

USE

- We use the passive form when the receiver of the action is more important than the performer of the action or when the performer of the action is not someone specific. The use of the passive avoids sentences with a vague subject like 'Someone' or 'Some people':
The local cinema ***was closed down*** *three years ago.*
Very few typewriters ***are being sold*** *these days.*
Children should ***be warned*** *not to speak to strangers.*
The 10.30 flight to Greece ***has been delayed****.*
- The use of the passive is a way of avoiding placing responsibility for a particular action on any specific person or organisation:
Due to the company's need to increase production, the lunch break ***will be reduced*** *from one hour to forty-five minutes.*

(The managers will probably prefer to say this than to say *We / The Company / The management will reduce the lunch break...*)

I am sorry that your letter ***was mislaid****.*
(The speaker may prefer not to say *I am sorry that I mislaid your letter.*)

- The passive is often used to avoid a change of subject in a sentence:
  When they got to the police station, they ***were*** *immediately* ***questioned****.*
  I went by train and ***was met*** *at the station by my aunt.*

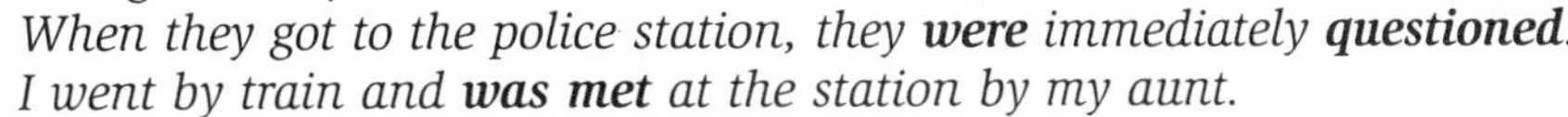

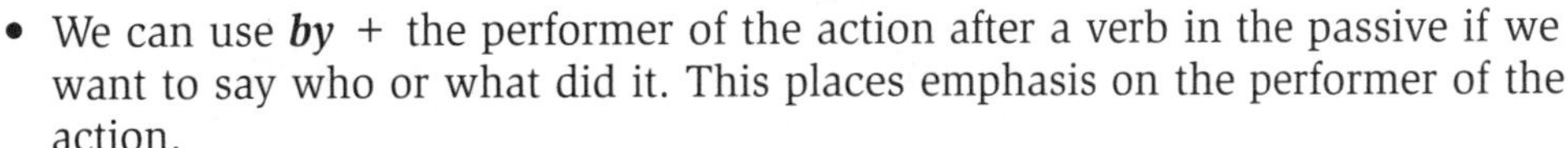

- We can use ***by*** + the performer of the action after a verb in the passive if we want to say who or what did it. This places emphasis on the performer of the action.
  We often use ***by*** + agent after the passive form of these verbs:
  build, compose, damage, design, discover, invent, make, write:
  The play was written ***by*** *a previously unknown author.*
  St. Paul's Cathedral was designed ***by*** *Christopher Wren.*
  The book tells how he was often beaten ***by*** *his cruel father.*
  The petition was signed ***by*** *all the people in the street.*
  We were stopped ***by*** *the police on our way home.*

- The passive is often used with verbs of saying and believing in these constructions:
  It + passive + that clause:
  It is expected that *many more people will die from starvation in the next decade.*

  There + passive + ***to be***:
  There are believed to be *many thousands of homeless teenagers living on the streets of the capital.*

  Subject + passive + ***to***–infinitive
  She is considered to be *the best singer in the group.*

- The passive is often used in notices, news reports and descriptions of processes:
  Customers ***are advised*** *to buy their tickets in advance.*
  Two escaped prisoners ***were recaptured*** *this morning when they tried to board an aircraft.*
  ENGLISH ***SPOKEN*** *HERE*
  The oranges ***are treated*** *with wax and then* ***stored*** *in large boxes before* ***being shipped*** *abroad.*

Notes

- Some languages often use an impersonal pronoun where English uses the passive. ***One*** as an impersonal pronoun is only occasionally used in formal English now. ***You*** is a more informal personal pronoun and is used more frequently than ***one***:
  One *often sees /* ***You*** *often see large cruise ships coming into this port.*
- ***Get*** is often used with certain past participles: *get engaged, get married, get lost, get killed, get dressed, get elected, get hit, get drunk.*

Practice

23a Rewrite the sentences, putting the underlined verbs into the passive. Make any other changes necessary.

1 They should have given us this information ages ago.

This information should have been given to us ages ago.

2 Do you want someone to wake you up in the morning?

Do you want to be woken up in the morning?

3 I don't like someone telling me what to do.

....

4 The windows are really dirty: no-one's cleaned them for weeks.

....

....

5 After the company made him redundant, he became very depressed.

....

....

6 I would like them to have given me the chance to explain my point of view, but they weren't interested.

....

....

7 I'm hoping they will choose me for the college football team.

....

....

8 People believe that many more people will die of skin cancer over the next ten years.

....

....

9 If it hadn't rained so much, we would have finished the job on time.

....

....

10 We can't take the car: the people at the garage are repairing it.

....

....

23b In your notebook, rewrite the following texts, putting the underlined verbs into the passive and making any other changes that are necessary. Use ***by*** + agent where appropriate.

1 The company is sorry to announce that the situation has forced it to introduce a range of cost-cutting measures as from the beginning of the new year. Unfortunately, we can no longer provide free tea and coffee. Someone is going to install new coin-operated drinks machines in every department and you can purchase a wide range of drinks from these. We will also stop overtime payments after the end of this month and we will expect all members of staff to complete their duties within their contract hours. You must no longer make personal calls from office phones and we request you to use the pay phone in the basement for this purpose.

2 Fire almost completely destroyed the Royal Hotel last night. By the time someone called the Fire Brigade, the hotel was already blazing. Ambulances took fifteen people to hospital suffering from severe burns. They say that seven of them are in a serious condition. People think that a discarded cigarette started the fire.

Example:
The Royal Hotel was almost completely destroyed by fire last night. By the time the Fire Brigade was/were called, ...

3 Jane is talking to her friend Greg about her holiday.

G: So, how was the holiday?
J: Oh, it was fantastic. They organized everything so well. As soon as we arrived at the airport, our courier met us and took us to the hotel. Someone had cleaned all the rooms beautifully and put fresh flowers on the tables.
G: Oh, how lovely. And what about the food?
J: It was excellent. They freshly prepared it all in the hotel and they even made the bread in the hotel kitchen. They served the bread rolls hot every morning with breakfast.
G: Mm, it does sound good. I must say, I'd like someone to cook my meals for me for a couple of weeks. And what about the surrounding area? Was that nice?
J: Oh beautiful. There were trips every day and they showed us all the local sights. There was so much history to see. You'd love it there, honestly.

4 Last month the Council put forward a plan to make the seafront traffic-free. Many of the shop and restaurant owners support the plan as they believe that a more pleasant environment will improve their trade. However, the hotel owners are less enthusiastic and say that the traffic restriction will make access to their car parks very difficult. There have also been protests from some local residents who complain that the closure of the seafront road will make their journeys around the town much longer.

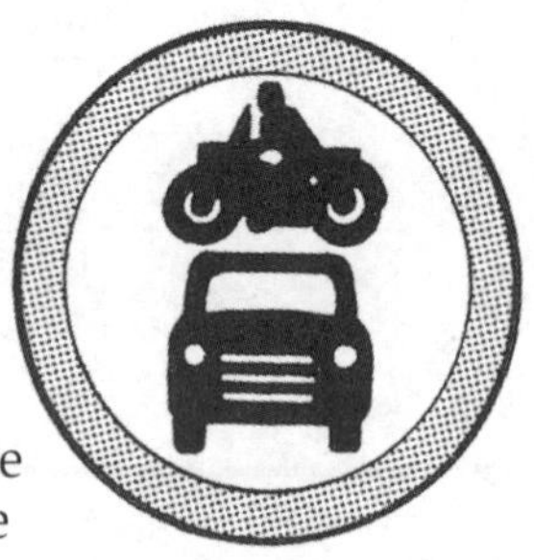

23c Put the verbs in brackets into the correct tense and form. Some of the verbs should be in the passive and some in the active. Write the answers in the spaces provided below the text.

Animals on the roads

More cars and lorries [1]..... (drive) on our roads every year and, sadly, as a result of this, more and more wild animals [2]..... (kill) by vehicles. Roads often [3]..... (cross) the routes that [4]..... (take) by animals when they are migrating, breeding or feeding.

Every spring, many thousands of toads [5]..... (kill) as they [6]..... (make) their way to the traditional breeding ponds. All over the world, animals are victims of the road and their dead remains can [7]..... (often see) lying on the roadside. Many badgers and hedgehogs [8]..... (hit) by cars at night as they [9]..... (move around) in search of food. Rabbits sometimes seem to [10]..... (hypnotize) by the headlights of cars and [11]..... (not move) quickly out of the way. Birds [12]..... (sometimes hit) too as they [13]..... (fly) low over roads.

[14]..... (can anything do) to protect these animals from the dangers of the road? Well, in 1969, a toad tunnel [15]..... (build) in Switzerland and was a great success. Since then, other tunnels [16]..... (construct) elsewhere in Europe, not just for toads but for badgers and salamanders too. In Florida, where the rare Florida panther [17]..... (live), panther tunnels [18]..... (build) under the highway and fencing [19]..... (put up) beside the highway to guide the animals safely into these underpasses. Road signs warning drivers to [20]..... (look out) for particular animals [21]..... (often see) in the US and it is to [22]..... (hope) that they [23]..... (become) a more common sight on the roads of Europe.

1 *are being driven* ....
2 ....
3 ....
4 ....
5 ....
6 ....
7 ....
8 ....
9 ....
10 ....
11 ....
12 ....
13 ....
14 ....
15 ....
16 ....
17 ....
18 ....
19 ....
20 ....
21 ....
22 ....
23 ....

24 The causative *have* and the causative *get*

FORM

have/get + *object* + *past participle*

USE

- We use the causative ***have*** or the causative ***get*** when we are not concerned about the person doing the action.
  The subject of the verb ***have*** or ***get*** causes the action to take place:
  We ***have/get*** *the windows cleaned once a month.*
  (We have an agreement with the window cleaner that s/he cleans the windows once a month and we pay him/her.)
  You should ***have/get*** *your eyes tested.* (You should arrange for an eye test.)
- We occasionally use the causative ***have*** or ***get*** with ***by*** + agent:
  We ***had/got*** *the house decorated by a local firm of decorators.*

Contrast: *have* and *get*

The causative ***have*** and the causative ***get*** are very similar and often interchangeable. However, the causative ***get*** is more concerned with the arranging that is required in order for something to be done:
I ***had*** *the car serviced this morning.*
(I caused this to happen but I may or may not have taken the car to the garage myself.)
I ***got*** *the car serviced this morning.*
(This is almost the same but there is an assumption here that I took the car to the garage.)
When we are concerned with the process of something happening and not the preparatory arrangements, we use the causative ***have*** and not the causative ***get***:
I like ***having*** *my hair done.*
They stayed with us while they were ***having*** *their flat decorated.*

We do not generally use the causative ***get*** in the present perfect or past perfect:
*Oh, you've **had** your hair done.* (NOT ~~*You've got your hair done*~~.)

Notes

- We also sometimes use ***get*** + object + past participle to say that we did something ourselves. When we use it in this way, it suggests that there was a lot to be done or that it was difficult but that we managed to finish it:
  *I **got** all my work done yesterday.*
- We occasionally use the causative ***have*** and ***get*** when the subject of ***have/get*** does not cause the action to happen but is an unwilling victim. It is generally used in this way with verbs denoting crimes:
  *I **had/got** my bag stolen last week.*

Practice

24 Rewrite the words underlined using ***have*** or ***get*** + object + past participle.

1 There's a photographer over there. Why don't we ask her to take our picture?
Why don't we have/get our picture taken?

2 I've finally decided to arrange for someone to pierce my nose.
I've finally decided to have/get my nose pierced.

3 There's a leak in the roof. We should arrange for someone to repair it.
....

4 What time is it? I'm afraid someone hasn't repaired my watch yet.
....
....

5 Someone is going to redecorate the kitchen for us next month.
....
....

6 If I were you, I'd ask someone to fell that tree. It shuts out all the light.
....

7 I'm having a bit of trouble with my eyes at the moment so someone's going to test them next week.
....
....

8 I love someone massaging my shoulders.
....

9 The dentist hasn't checked my teeth this year.
....

10 The baby was crying because <u>someone was washing her hair</u>.

....

11 He looks much younger. <u>I think someone's dyed his hair</u>.

....

12 I don't know if I've passed the course because <u>the tutors haven't marked all my work yet</u>.

....

13 That wasps' nest is dangerous. <u>You must ask someone to remove it</u>.

....

MISCELLANEOUS

25 Constructions after *wish*

USE

- With past simple.
  To express dissatisfaction with a present situation or repeated habitual activity, use ***wish*** + past simple:
  *I **wish** she <u>didn't</u>...* (but she does)
  *I **wish** she <u>did</u>...* (but she doesn't)
  *I **wish** she <u>spoke</u> French.* (but she doesn't. I would very much like her to.)
  With the verb ***to be***, use ***was*** or ***were*** after ***I/She/He/It. Were*** is a little more formal:
  *I **wish** the weather <u>was/were</u> a bit warmer.* (but it isn't)
- With ***would***.
  To express dissatisfaction and annoyance about something that we would like to be different but that we do not expect to be different.
  When we use it to refer to a person, it suggests that the person refuses to change:
  *I **wish** she <u>would</u> speak French.* (but she won't. She can speak French but she refuses to speak it.)
  *I **wish** it <u>would</u> stop raining.* (but it won't. I do not expect it to stop.)
- With past perfect.
  To express regret about the past, use ***wish*** + *past perfect*:
  *I **wish** I <u>had studied</u> harder.* (but I didn't and now I regret it.)

Notes

- We can use ***if only...*** in place of ***I wish...*** . It also expresses dissatisfaction and regret. It is somewhat stronger than ***wish***: *If only I hadn't said that.*
- ***Wish*** + ***to***-infinitive is a more formal way of saying ***I want to...*** or ***I would like to...*** It is used in formal spoken language or in writing: *The management **wish** <u>to inform</u> you that...*

Practice

25 Rewrite the sentences using ***I wish*** + past simple, past perfect or ***would***.

1 I haven't got a car. I would very much like to have one.
I wish I had a car.

2 I went to bed late last night. I regret it now.
I wish I hadn't gone to bed late last night.

3 We don't live in a nice big flat. I would like us to.
....

4 I didn't buy that dress. I regret it now.
....

5 He won't stop shouting. I would like him to.
....

6 I lost my temper. I regret it now.
....

7 You didn't tell me the truth. I am very sorry that you didn't.
....

8 You're playing that music. I would like you to stop playing it but I don't expect that you will.
....

9 I didn't go to that concert. I regret it now.
....

10 I don't have an interesting job. I would like my job to be more interesting.
....

11 My family live a long way from here. I would like them to live nearer to me.
....

12 You're not listening to me. I feel annoyed about it and I would like you to listen to me but I don't think you will.
....

13 I am not with him now. I would very much like to be.
....

14 I spent all my money on that new coat. I regret it now.
....

15 I'm really hungry now. We didn't eat before we came out and I regret that.
....

26 Phrasal verbs

A phrasal verb is formed with a verb + particle. The particle is an adverb or a preposition. Sometimes its meaning may be inferred from the meaning of the verb and the particle, e.g. *Can you **slow down**?*, but often the meaning is completely different from the meanings of the separate words, e.g. *He **takes after** his mother in his mathematical ability.*

Types of phrasal verbs:

- Intransitive:
  *We must **set off** early tomorrow.*

- Transitive (separable):
  The object can go *before* or *after* the particle.
  *Did you **turn down** that job offer?*
  *Did you **turn** that job offer **down**?*
  *Did you **turn** it **down**?*
  (NOT ~~*Did you **turn down** it?*~~)

- Transitive (inseparable):
  The object can only go *after* the particle.
  *She **takes after** her mother.*
  (NOT ~~*She **takes** her mother **after**.*~~)

Notes

- Some phrasal verbs have three words: verb + adverb + preposition. In three-word phrasal verbs, the object can only go *after* the preposition:
  *She **came up with** lots of good ideas.*
  *I think you should **get down to** your work.*
- Some combinations of verb + particle have more than one meaning and some of them may be either transitive or intransitive:
  *Business was very slow over the winter but it's **picking up** now.*
  *I'll **pick** you **up** at 8 o'clock.*
- Many verbs are followed by prepositions but are not phrasal verbs. The combination of the verb with the preposition does not have a meaning of its own. The verb and the preposition each have their literal meaning:
  *She **walked** through the room.*
  *I don't **approve** of this idea.*

  The distinction between a phrasal verb and a prepositional verb is not important, however. It is only important to understand the meaning of the verbs.

Practice

26a Underline the phrasal verbs in the following dialogue. Copy the table into your notebook and write the phrasal verbs in the infinitive in the appropriate columns.

Intransitive	*Transitive (separable)*	*Transitive (inseparable)*
get on		

Jerry, a head of department, is talking to his manager, Tony.

T: So can you tell me how things are going in your department at the moment, Jerry?

J: Well, Alison's <u>getting on</u> very well. I think we did the right thing taking her on. She's already achieved higher sales than Martin this month. She's got lots of enthusiasm and she never wastes any time; she just gets on with it.
T: Well, that's good news. But what about Martin? Is his work still not coming up to standard?
J: No, it isn't. His sales figures have been going down steadily since the beginning of the year. If he carries on like this, I think I'll have to take him off that job and put him back in the office.
T: So what do you think the problem is?
J: Well, to be honest, I think he's lost enthusiasm for the job. And I think his outside interests are taking up a lot of his time and energy.
T: I'm afraid that's just not good enough. If his sales figures don't start going up soon, he might find himself looking round for another job.
J: Yes, I think that's right. I'll fix up a meeting with him so that we can run through this year's figures and then I'll let him know that he can't get away with this poor performance for much longer.
T: Yes, I really think he should give up some of these outside activities if his work is suffering.
J: Yes, I agree. Don't worry, I'll sort it out with him.

26b Rewrite the parts underlined, replacing the words in bold with a phrasal verb from Exercise 26a.

1 I'd like to discuss your plans with you. <u>Can we **arrange** to have a meeting soon</u>?

Can we fix up a meeting soon?

2 You've got exams soon. <u>You can't **continue** going out every night</u>.

....

3 He arrives late for work every day. <u>I don't know how he **does it without getting into trouble**</u>.

....

4 If the business continues to expand, <u>we'll need to **employ** more staff soon</u>.

....

....

5 <u>We'll never get this problem **resolved** if we don't talk about it</u>.

....

....

6 <u>The club membership has been **declining** for the last five years</u>.

....

....

7 <u>I'm going to **remove** you from this case, detective</u>. I think you're becoming too personally involved.

....

8 I really think he should **stop** drinking; it's not doing him any good.

....

9 I'm afraid I'm a bit disappointed with the course. It hasn't really **reached** my expectations.

....

10 I don't think she'll want to be in the play this year. Her new job is **using** all her energy.

....

26c Complete the gaps with the following phrasal verbs. Put the verbs into the correct tense and form. **Two** of the verbs should be put into the passive. Write the answers in the spaces provided below the text.

turn up	put in for	pick up	run out of	come down	go on
turn down	save up	~~take over~~	live off	cheer up	fall back on

3, Fir Close,
Poole.
April 6th

Dear Chris,

How's life treating you these days? Things haven't been too good for me lately, I'm afraid. My company [1].... by UK Confectionery in January and half the workforce was made redundant, including me. I [2].... lots of different jobs since then but I [3].... every time. I think I might have to retrain, but the problem is that I [4].... money now so I can't afford to pay for a course. I've already spent all the money I [5].... to go on holiday and I've got no other money to [6].... . I really hope that something [7].... soon otherwise I don't know what I'll do. I know the government keeps saying that the economy's starting to [8].... now but I don't see any signs of it myself. And it's just so difficult trying to [9].... social security.

Anyway, sorry to be so depressing. I just hope I have some better news for you when I next see you. In fact, I was wondering if you'd like to [10].... for a weekend soon. It would [11].... me .... to see you again and I promise I won't [12]....

1 *was taken over*............ 7 ....

2 .... 8 ....

3 .... 9 ....

4 .... 10 ....

5 .... 11 ....

6 .... 12 ....

Conditionals

27 First, second and third conditional

There are three main types of conditional sentences.

First conditional (or Type 1 conditional)

If I ***see*** *Andrew at the meeting, I* ***'ll give*** *him your message.*
present simple — future simple

To talk about something that is quite likely to happen in the future. It is very possible that I will see Andrew at the meeting, in which case I'll give him your message. The condition is quite likely to be fulfilled.

Second conditional (or Type 2 conditional)

If my parents ***were*** *alive, they* ***would be*** *very proud of me now.*
[*they'****d***]
past simple — *would* + infinitive

To talk about a present situation which is impossible: a hypothetical situation. The condition cannot be fulfilled because my parents are not alive.

If she ***changed*** *her job, she* ***would be*** *much happier.*
[*she'****d***]

To talk about a future event that is unlikely to happen. The speaker does not expect her to change her job. That is, it is unlikely that the condition will be fulfilled.

Third conditional (or Type 3 conditional)

If she ***had worked*** *harder, she* ***would have passed*** *the exams.*
[*she'****d have*** / *she* ***would've***]
past perfect — *would* + perfect infinitive

To talk about something in the past that did not happen. She didn't work harder and she didn't pass her exams. It is an unfulfilled condition in the past.

Notes

- In conditional sentences, the conditional clause can be the first or second clause in the sentence, although it is more often the first clause.
  When the conditional clause comes first, it is followed by a comma. When it comes second, there is no comma.
  If I get home early enough, I'll make a special dinner.
  I'll make a special dinner if I get home early enough.
- The tense and verb forms given here are the ones most commonly used in conditional sentences. However, it is possible to use other tenses and these variations are presented on pages 85-86.

Practice

27 The following sentences are first, second or third conditional. Put the verbs in brackets into the appropriate form.

1 We wanted to go out yesterday but the weather was terrible. If it *had been* (be) a nice day, we *would have gone* (go) for a picnic.

2 Why don't you explain everything to him? If you .... (not tell) him the truth, I'm sure you .... (regret) it one day.

3 Jennifer was here not long ago. If you .... (come round) earlier, you .... (see) her.

4 Apparently, the ferry company are planning to close the port in this town. If that .... (happen), the town .... (lose) a great deal of money.

5 I .... (help) you with it if I .... (have) more time but I'm afraid I haven't got any spare time at all at the moment.

6 The government is expecting to win the next election, but if it .... (lose), the Prime Minister .... (resign) from politics.

7 I am so glad that you took me to your friend's party. If we .... (not go) there, I .... (never meet) Adrian.

8 It's ridiculous that trains are so expensive. If fares .... (be) cheaper, I'm sure more people .... (use) the train and leave their cars at home.

9 If she .... (get) that job she's applied for, she .... (be) delighted. And I think she's got a good chance of getting it.

10 Fortunately the explosion took place at night when the streets were empty. It .... (be) a disaster if it .... (happen) in the middle of the day.

11 The talks between the two leaders keep breaking down. If they .... (break down) again, it is possible that there .... (be) a war between the two countries.

12 If Alison .... (know) anything about car mechanics, I'm sure she .... (help) us fix the car, but I think she knows even less than we do.

13 They've been married for twenty years now but I don't think she .... (marry) him if she .... (know) what a selfish man he was.

14 Children spend too much time watching television and playing computer games. I'm sure they .... (be) happier if they .... (spend) more time playing outside.

15 Jamie has everything he wants but he's always moaning. I'm sure that if I .... (have) so much money, I .... (not moan) all the time.

28 Conditional sentences: variations in tenses

There are a number of variations in the tenses or verb forms that can be used in conditional sentences.

First conditional

The ***if*** clause is usually in the present simple. However, we can also use: present continuous, present perfect simple, present perfect continuous, ***can***, ***should***:

If he**'s** still **waiting** for you, he'll be very angry.
If you**'re coming out** with us tonight, you'll need to be ready by 7 o'clock.
If Rob**'s received** your letter, I'm sure he'll phone you today.
If it**'s been raining** in the night, you'll have to wear wellingtons.
If I **can finish** work early, I'll come and help you.
If I **should see** him, I'll tell him the good news.

Note: When we use ***if*** + ***should***, the condition is less likely to be fulfilled.

The main clause usually has the verb in the future with ***will/shall***. However, we can also use: 'be going to' future, future continuous, future perfect, imperative, ***can/could***, ***may/might***, ***should/ought to***, ***must***:

If Helen passes all her exams, we**'re going to buy** her a big present.
If we book this holiday, we**'ll be lying** on a warm beach in two weeks' time.
If they win this next match, they**'ll have won** every match in the season.
If you need any help, **call** me.
If you phone me after 12 o'clock, I **might be** in bed.
If they don't eat their dinner, they **can't have** any ice-cream.

Second conditional

The ***if*** clause is usually in the past simple. However, we can also use the past continuous, ***could,*** or ***were/was to***:

If you **were coming** with me, I'd give you a lift.
If I **could have** the day off, I'd come with you.
If you **were to** ask Steve, I'm sure he would do it.

The main clause usually has the modal ***would*** + infinitive. However, the modals ***could*** and ***might*** are also used and the infinitive can be in the continuous form:

If we had more money, we **wouldn't be living** here.
If we had more money, we **could go out** more often.
If you asked Tony, he **might do** it for you.

Third conditional

The *if* clause is usually in the past perfect simple. However, we can also use the past perfect continuous or ***could*** + perfect infinitive:

If he **had been travelling** in that car, he would have been killed too.
If we **could have** got a taxi, we would have come round to see you.

The main clause usually has the modal ***would*** + perfect infinitive. However, we can also use the modals ***could*** and ***might*** before the perfect infinitive:

If I had known there was no more work to do, I **could have stayed** in bed.
If the ambulance had come sooner, he **might have been saved**.

The zero conditional

If I **stay** out late, I always **get** a taxi home.
present simple   present simple

To describe something that is generally true. The use of ***if*** here is very similar to ***when***.

Each time I stay out late, I get a taxi home.

We can also use the past simple in the two clauses:
If I **stayed** out late, I always **got** a taxi home.

Practice

28 Put the verbs in brackets into the appropriate form.

1 Oh dear, I think we're a bit late. If the concert's already started, we *won't be allowed* (not be allowed) to go in.

2 He wouldn't be coming here if he .... (not want) to.

3 If you were planning to leave your husband, I .... (advise) you against it.

4 He could be earning lots of money now if he really .... (want) to, but I don't think that's what he wants.

5 You can stay here tonight if you .... (not have) anywhere else to stay.

6 If I could have phoned you, I .... (tell) you what was happening.

7 If you .... (have) any problems, give me a ring.

8 If you .... (get) here at about 8 o'clock, I'll be waiting for you.

9 We could have got there in time if you .... (phone) us earlier.

10 If this should happen again, ... (come) and .... (tell) me about it immediately.

11 You can't expect kindness and support from your family if you .... (not give) the same to them.

12 If she's been working all day, she .... (be) very tired when she gets in.

13 If the management were to reinstate the strike leader, the strike .... (be called off).

14 If I .... (keep) working on this essay, I'll have finished it by tonight.

15 If I could borrow some money, I .... (definitely come) on the holiday with you, but I think it's unlikely.

16 I might have been able to help you if you .... (explain) the problem to me.

17 If I could live wherever I wanted to, I think I .... (choose) to live on a Scottish island.

18 If they had been listening more carefully, they .... (might understand) what I was saying.

19 If I .... (be) a year older, I could join the army.

20 If I .... (get) a pay rise, I'm going to buy a new car.

29 Mixed conditionals

In addition to all the tense variations that we can use in first, second and third conditionals, it is also possible to mix conditionals so that, for example, the ***if*** clause uses a verb form used in the first conditional and the main clause uses a verb form used in the third conditional. The context defines the meaning. The most common mixed conditional is:

3rd	2nd
if + past perfect	***would/could/might*** + infinitive

Examples of mixed conditionals

3rd / 2nd
If I **had worked** harder at university, I **would have** a degree now.

1st / 2nd
If you **come** to the party tomorrow, I **wouldn't bring** Mike with you.

2nd / 3rd
If she **loved** him, she **would have stayed** with him.

Practice

29 Match the clauses and write the mixed conditional sentences in your notebook.

1 If you had told me about this problem earlier,	A he probably won't be at the meeting.
2 If you were a more sensitive person,	B you could always ring them up.
3 If they don't contact you soon,	C his wife would never have left him.
4 If he hadn't died so young,	D you wouldn't have said that to her.
5 If he didn't work so hard all the time,	E I would have had them by now.
6 If the train hadn't been delayed,	F everything would be all right now.
7 If he was feeling ill this morning,	G would you hurry up and get ready?
8 If you're coming with us,	H you wouldn't be so busy this month.
9 If I really wanted to have children,	I we would be there by now.
10 If you had worked harder last month,	J I'm sure he'd be a famous musician by now.

Example:
1F – *If you had told me about this problem earlier, everything would be all right now.*

30 Conditionals

As you have seen, it is possible to use almost any combination of tenses in conditional sentences. The context determines the choice of tense.

Check

30 Put the verbs in brackets into the appropriate form.

1 Harry and Sarah, a husband and wife, are talking.

H: Shall I make the children something to eat?

S: I wouldn't bother. You know how much they eat when they visit their grandparents.

H: That's true. If they [1] *have been eating* (eat) all afternoon, they [2] .... (not want) anything when they get home.

S: Are we going to pick them up soon?

H: No, my parents are bringing them over. We agreed that if I [3] .... (take) them there, they [4] .... (bring) them back.

S: Oh good. Well, if we [5] .... (not collect) them, I [6] .... (go back) upstairs and do a bit more work. I've nearly finished that report now. If I [7] .... (do) another half hour's work, I [8] .... (finish) it by the time the children get home.

H: Why do you always have to bring work home with you? If you [9] .... (not agree) to take on that new job, you [10] .... (have) much more free time now.

S: Yes, and if I [11] .... (not take on) that job, we [12] .... (not have) much money now.

H: That's true, but I don't like you working so much.

S: Well never mind. We've got a week's holiday soon. Just think! In two weeks' time, we [13] .... (lie) on a warm sunny beach – that's if I [14] .... (can get) the time off work of course.

H: What do you mean, 'if'?

S: Well, everything's very busy at the moment. And if we [15]... (get) any more orders, I just [16]... (not see) how I can leave the office.

H: What? But that's ridiculous.

2 Dear Angela,

Thanks for your letter, it was nice to hear from you. And yes, I would like to come and see you in Spain. If I [17]... (save up) enough money when the summer holidays start, I [18]... (try) and come then – if that [19]... (be) O.K. Otherwise, I'll come over in the autumn because I'm sure I [20]... (save up) enough by October – if I [21]... (not lose) my job by then! Unfortunately, lots of people in our company are being made redundant and it could be me next. If I [22]... (have) any sense, I [23]... (leave) this job ages ago. Still it could be worse I suppose.

I was delighted to hear about your promotion – it's great news. If you [24]... (keep on) getting promoted, you [25]... (run) the whole school soon.

And it sounds like the weather's been really good over there. It's been terrible here. I don't think it's been dry once this month. If it [26]... (be) dry, I [27]... (not notice). Oh well, we're hoping it'll get better soon. If it [28]... (still rain) at the weekend, we

[29] .... (decide) we'll try and emigrate!

Have you heard from Charlotte by the way? She said she was going to phone you to tell you that she's pregnant. If she [30] .... (not phone you up yet), [31] .... (not tell) her that I've already told you her news, will you?

All the best,

Jade

31 Words other than *if*

Conditionals can also be introduced by the following conjunctions:

unless	even if	if only	as/so long as	assuming(that)
on (the) condition (that)	provided/providing (that)			
In questions: suppose/supposing (that)	what if	imagine		

Practice

31 In your notebook, rewrite the sentences replacing *if* with the most appropriate conjunction.

1 Mr Davidson says he'll come and give a talk at the conference if we pay him a reasonable fee.
(supposing that / unless / on condition that)
Mr Davidson says he'll come and give a talk at the conference on condition that we pay him a reasonable fee.

2 I won't help him if he doesn't ask me properly.
(provided / unless / as long as)

3 If I could get a job, life here would be perfect.
(what if / even if / if only)

4 If you had a lot of money, do you think you would give up work?
(Supposing that / Providing that / As long as)

5 If the train arrives on time, they'll be here in a few minutes.
(What if / Assuming that / On condition that)

6 If he doesn't agree to my request, what will I do then?
(Imagine / What if / Provided that)

7 You can go out tonight if you get back by midnight.
(as long as / assuming that / supposing that)

8 If the helicopter hadn't been there to save her, what would have happened then?
(If only / Imagine / Unless)
9 If you'd offered to pay me a thousand pounds, I wouldn't have done it.
(If only / Provided that / Even if)
10 If Rosie gets this new promotion, we'll have enough money for a holiday abroad this year.
(Even if / Provided that / Supposing that)

32 Implied conditionals

Conditions are not always expressed in the form of conditional clauses, particularly in spoken English. They can be expressed in another way or they may be evident from the context:

Please come out with us tonight. I'm sure you'll enjoy it.
(implied condition: *if you come out with us*)
With a bit more help, I would have finished it on time.
(*with a bit more help* = if I had had more help)
I'm sure we'd really enjoy going on holiday with you but we just can't afford it.
(implied condition: *if we went*)
I'm glad you didn't tell Matthew about it. He would have been furious.
(implied condition: *if you had told him*)

Practice

32 The condition is not stated in a conditional clause in the following underlined sentences. It is implied or is stated in a different way. Write a sentence containing the underlined words as a main clause, and an appropriate conditional clause.

1 I think Alison should apply for the job. She would make a very good managing director.

She would make a very good managing director if she got the job.

2 The problem is that she doesn't work very hard. I know that she could do really well.

....

....

3 We're lucky it's sunny today. It would be horrible sitting out here otherwise.

....

....

4 He would not be able to live on his own without the help of his neighbours.

....

....

5 With luck, we'll finish the job by the end of today.

....

....

6 I hear you're thinking of going to Indonesia for the summer. You'll love it there.

....

7 I hope those refugees aren't deported, but I think they will be. They may be imprisoned or even executed.

....

....

8 It's a good job you brought all those tables and chairs in from outside last night. The rain would have ruined them.

....

....

9 Mark should have told her the truth. I'm sure she would have forgiven him.

....

....

10 Without the help of the Red Cross doctors, many more would have died.

....

....

Modal auxiliaries

33 Modal auxiliaries: introduction

Modal auxiliaries are also sometimes called modal verbs or modals.
The following are modal auxiliaries:

Present	*Past form*
can	could
may	might
will	would
shall	should
must	—
ought to	—
need	—

FORM

- Positive: subject + modal + bare infinitive:
  *I **must** see you tomorrow.*
  *We **must** go now.*
- Negative: subject + modal + ***not/n't*** + bare infinitive:
  *You **shouldn't** go to bed so late.*
  *They **needn't** come if they don't want to.*
- Question: modal + subject + bare infinitive:
  ***Can** you help me?*
  ***Will** she be here soon?*
- Short answers: subject + modal auxiliary:
  *Yes, we **can**. No, they **won't**.*
- Modal auxiliaries always stay the same.
  They cannot be:
  - put into different tenses.
  - used as infinitives.
  - used as gerunds or present participles.
- They can be followed by the infinitive in different forms:

	Active	*Passive*
modal +	*bare infinitive*: must **take**	***be*** + *past participle*: must **be taken**
	be + *present participle*: must **be taking**	
	have + *past participle*: must **have taken**	***have been*** + *past participle*: must **have been taken**
	have been + *present participle*: must **have been taking**	

Notes

- **need** can be a modal auxiliary only in the question or negative form.
- **ought** is the only modal auxiliary followed by ***to***.
- **dare** can be used as a modal auxiliary in the question and negative forms. It can also be used as a main verb followed by the ***to***-infinitive.
  It is not a common modal auxiliary and is not therefore included in the practice exercises.

Practice

33 Rewrite the following sentences using a modal. The underlined words can be written as subject + modal + verb (or modal + subject + verb in questions). In some sentences, more than one modal is possible.

1 I promise to phone you next week.

I will/I'll phone you next week.

2 At the age of nine, he still didn't know how to read.

At the age of nine, he still couldn't read.

3 It's essential that we leave on time tomorrow morning.

....

....

4 Are you able to come with me tonight?

....

5 It's not a good idea for you to work so hard.

....

6 It's possible that they'll be here soon.

....

7 Why don't we go and see a film tonight?

....

8 He said that he intended to write to me soon.

....

9 Is it possible for me to sit here?

....

10 <u>He refuses to give</u> me an answer.

....

11 <u>It's not necessary for you to apologize</u>.

....

12 <u>Am I allowed to smoke</u> in here?

....

13 <u>He knew how to speak</u> four languages by the time he was twelve.

....

....

14 I want to help you but <u>I'm not able to</u>.

....

15 I think <u>it's a good idea for me to stay in</u> tonight: I've got a lot of work to do.

....

....

16 I don't know who she is but <u>it's possible that she's</u> Rick's sister.

....

....

17 <u>Do not tell him</u> any of this: it's vital that it remains a secret

....

....

18 <u>I intend to finish</u> this essay before I go to bed.

....

....

19 It's 7 o'clock. <u>I assume that Clare will be</u> here soon.

....

....

20 He's in but he's not answering the phone. <u>I'm sure that he's</u> asleep.

....

....

34 Ability: *can, could, be able*

- ***Can*** (present or future) and ***could*** (past) refer to a general ability to do something. ***Can*** is also used to refer to an ability to do something specific at a time in the future:
  *She **can** sing really well.*
  *I **can** come and see you next week.*
  *I **can't** swim so I won't come to the pool with you.*
  *He **could** read when he was four.*
  *I **couldn't** understand the language when I first came here.*

- ***Can*** and ***could*** refer to the ability to do something, but not to the doing of it. We use ***can*** or ***be able*** to talk about ability:
  *Will you **be able** to/**Can** you come on Saturday?*
  *My parents live quite a distance away so we**'re not able** to/**can't** see them very often.*
  *He had a motorbike accident at the age of eighteen and after that he **wasn't able** to/**couldn't** walk.*

  We use ***be able*** to talk about ability + achievement of the action:
  *Jan gave me a lift home so I **was able** to stay at the party till late.*
  *We got lost but we **were able** to find our way home again with the map.*

- We use ***will be able*** and not ***can*** to talk about skills that will be acquired in the future:
  ***I'll be able** to drive by next summer so we can hire a car.*
  ***Will** you **be able** to read textbooks in German when you've finished this course?*

- We use ***can*** + ***be*** + adjective or noun to talk about possibility:
  *The sea **can be** quite warm in September./The sea is sometimes quite warm in September.*
  *She **can be** very charming when she wants to be.*

- We use ***be able*** for different grammatical forms that are not possible with ***can***:
  *I like **being able** to work at home.*
  *We'd like **to be able** to help you but we can't.*
  ***I've been able** to work much faster since I got that new computer.*

- We use ***can, could*** and ***could have*** in conditional sentences. We also use them in sentences with an implied condition:
  *I **can** help you if you want me to.*
  *I **could** do it if I had the time.*
  *You **could** do that job easily. (if you had that job)*
  *I **couldn't have** done it if I hadn't had your help.*
  *I **could have** got here earlier but I didn't know you were waiting. (I could have got here earlier if I had known you were waiting.)*

Practice

34 Complete the sentences with the correct form of ***can***, ***could*** or ***be able***. If it is possible to use ***can/could*** or ***be able***, use ***can/could***.

1 He is very fit for his age. He .*can run*. (run) really fast.

2 I'd like ..*to be able to work*. (work) with you one day.

3 He .... (not climb) up to the top: he was too scared.

4 If they hadn't phoned for an ambulance, he .... (die).

5 I love .... (spend) all morning in bed at the weekends.

6 We .... (go) to that concert tomorrow if the tickets haven't sold out.

7 I think you should go in the spring: it .... (be) very crowded there in the summer.

8 I .... (not understand) what he says: he speaks too quickly.

9 Do you know where Nick's glasses are? He .... (not see) very much without them.

10 .... (speak) another language fluently is a great advantage when you're looking for a job.

11 Jonathan .... (not say) anything until he was about three years old.

12 We .... (not phone her up) because her phone had broken, but fortunately we .... (get) a message to her.

13 Amy's exam results weren't very good. She .... (do) better.

14 I .... (not sleep) very well for the last four nights. It's been too hot.

15 She tried to think of other things but she .... (not put) that awful memory out of her mind.

16 You should .... (go out) when you want to.

17 .... (you come) to the party on Saturday?

18 I .... (ride) this bike soon: I just need more time to practise.

19 He doesn't do very much when he's here. He .... (be) more helpful.

20 I .... (play) tennis really well a few years ago, but not anymore.

35 Certainty, possibility, deduction: *can, could, may, might, must, will, should, ought to*

- To talk about something that it is possible to do at any time, use ***can*** or ***may***. With this use, ***can*** and ***may*** are often followed by the passive infinitive:
  Suitcases ***can/may*** *be left in the left luggage office at the station.*
  Stamps ***can/may*** *be bought at most shops which sell cards.*

- To talk about a future possibility, use ***may*** or ***might***. We can also use ***could***; ***could*** refers to a theoretical possibility:
  The parcel ***may/might*** *arrive tomorrow.*
  I ***may/might*** *see you next week.*
  You ***could*** *go by train. (It is possible to take a train there if you wanted to do that.)*

- To talk about a present or future certainty, use ***will*** + simple or continuous infinitive:
  *You can phone Sally: she'****ll*** *be at home now.*
  *I'****ll*** *be there by 9 o'clock.*
  The meeting ***will*** *start at 7.30.*
  *We should go now: they'****ll*** *be waiting for us.*
  *I'****ll*** *be standing on the platform when you arrive.*

- To talk about the possibility in the present, use ***may***, ***might*** or ***could*** + simple infinitive (usually the verb ***to be***) or continuous infinitive:
  'Where's Tony?' 'I don't know. He ***may*** *be outside.'*
  'Whose is this?' 'It ***could*** *be Emma's.'*
  Alison's not in the office today so she ***may*** *be working at home.*
  I won't phone Jennifer now because she ***might*** *be having a rest.*

- To talk about possibility in the past, use ***may***, ***might*** or ***could*** + perfect infinitive (simple or continuous):
  It's 8.30 so she ***may*** *have left by now.*
  I don't know why they're so late. I suppose they ***could*** *have got lost.*
  Sue wasn't at the party last night. She ***might*** *have been feeling too tired to come.*

- To make a deduction about something in the present, use ***must*** (positive deduction) or ***can't*** (negative deduction) + simple infinitive (usually the verb ***to be***) or continuous infinitive:
  Jane's not at home so she ***must*** *be on her way here.*
  The office is closed now so he ***can't*** *be there.*
  Barbara's back at work now so she ***must*** *be feeling better.*
  He ***can't*** *be driving here: he hasn't got a car.*

- To make a deduction about something in the past, use ***must*** or ***can't*** (or ***couldn't***) + perfect infinitive (simple or continuous):
  It's very wet outside so it ***must*** *have rained in the night.*
  He ***can't*** *have forgotten about the meeting: he talked to me about it only this morning.*
  You ***must*** *have been talking on the phone for a long time last night: I phoned four times and it was engaged.*
  Eddie ***couldn't*** *have done that robbery: he was with me the whole weekend.*

- We can use ***should*** or ***ought to*** + present infinitive to make assumptions about the present or the future and ***should*** or ***ought to*** + perfect infinitive to make assumptions about the past. We use ***should*** more frequently than ***ought to***:
  The train got in half an hour ago so they ***should*** *be here soon.*
  The sun's been shining all day so the sea ***should*** *be quite warm now.*
  The weather's lovely there at this time of year so they ***should*** *be having a nice holiday.*
  Let's go and see Cathy: she ***ought to*** *have finished working by now.*

Notes

- We can use modals in short responses:
  'Are they at home now?' 'They ***might*** *be.'*
  'I expect Debbie was very pleased with her results.' 'Yes, she ***must*** *have been.'*
- In short responses, ***do*** often replaces other verbs:
  'Has he gone home?' 'He may have ***done****.'*

Practice

35 Complete the sentences with ***can, could, may, might, will, should, ought to*** or ***must*** and an infinitive in the appropriate form.

1 Kerry's rather late. She *must have missed* (miss) the train.

2 Travellers' cheques *can/may be exchanged* (be exchanged) at most banks.

3 They're not answering the phone so they .... (be) out.

4 Don't phone her now. It .... (be) the middle of the night in Australia.

5 They .... (not move) house yet. I saw them in town this morning.

6 I haven't seen Molly this week. I think she .... (visit) her parents but I'm not sure.

7 Her exam results are coming out soon. She worked very hard so she .... (do) well.

8 That woman's just fallen over. Let's go and see her: she .... (be) hurt.

9 I don't know where she is. She .... (not still play) tennis: it's been dark for the last hour.

10 I sent the letter two days ago so he .... (get) it by now, but you can never be sure.

11 The encyclopaedias .... (be found) on the second floor of the library.

12 Jim's been very quiet since his girlfriend went away. He .... (miss) her.

13 I .... (come) and visit you at the weekend. Anyway, I'll give you a ring to let you know.

14 She was with a man I didn't recognize. It .... (be) her brother because he looked a bit like her.

15 The roads are fairly quiet today so we .... (have) a good journey.

16 'Do you think Josephine .... (be) at home now?'

'No, she .... She .... (have) a swim. She always does at this time in the morning.'

17 'Why do you think Tricia was in such a hurry?'

'I don't know. She .... (run) to catch the bus.'

18 These glasses .... (be) Tim's: they look a bit like his.

19 It .... (not rain): the ground's completely dry.

20 I .... (join) the sports club in the summer but I haven't decided yet.

21 What a terrible thing to have happened. You .... (be) terrified.

22 I told her you were coming so she .... (expect) you.

23 They've just rung the bell so the children .... (be) out of the classrooms in a minute.

24 That looks like Jack but it .... (not be) him. He went to live in Australia last year.

25 I've got a stomachache this morning. I .... (eat) too much last night or I .... (have) some sort of virus.

36 Advice, obligation, necessity: *should, ought to, must, have to, have got to, need*

- To give advice, use ***should*** or ***ought to***. ***Should*** is used more frequently.
  Should/Ought to = that course of action would be a good idea; it would be the best thing to do. It can refer to present time or to future time:
  You ***should/ought to*** *try and lose some weight.*
  We ***should/ought to*** *be leaving soon.*
  You ***shouldn't/oughtn't to*** *take any notice of him. He always upsets you.*
  Should *we/****Ought*** *we* ***to*** *tell Ann where we're going?*

  We often use ***should/ought to*** with *I think .../Do you think ...?/Don't you think...?*
  Don't you think you ***should/ought to*** *stop seeing him?*

  We sometimes use *I* ***should*** ... (NOT ~~*I* ***ought to***~~) to give advice to someone else when there is an implied condition *if I were you*:
  Everything's going to be allright. I ***should*** *stop worrying about it. (if I were you)*

- To give strong advice and recommendations, use ***must***. It can refer to present time or to future time.
  You ***must*** *go and see that film; it's fantastic.*
  You really ***must*** *try to forget him.*
  You ***mustn't*** *let him talk to you like that.*
  We ***must*** *go and visit them more often.*
  You ***must*** *come and stay with us sometime.* (Here it is used to give a casual invitation.)

- To criticize actions in the past, use ***should*** or ***ought to*** + perfect infinitive.
  Should/Ought to in the past means that the subject did not do the right thing:
  I ***should*** *have stayed at home.* (= I didn't stay at home and my behaviour was wrong.)
  You ***shouldn't*** *have said that.* (= You said that and it was the wrong thing to have said.)
  They ***shouldn't*** *have been talking when the exam started.*
  Should *I have phoned you back?*

- To talk about obligation, use ***must, mustn't*** or ***have to***.
  Have to is not a modal verb. It is an ordinary verb and it can be used in any form.
  Must and ***have to*** are often interchangeable but there is sometimes a difference between them.
  Have to – the obligation is often external, it comes from the situation:
  We ***have to*** *get up early tomorrow to catch the plane.*
  (The time of the plane is the reason for the obligation.)
  Must – the obligation comes from the speaker or writer of the sentence. This may be an individual or some kind of authority:
  We ***must*** *get up early tomorrow. We've got a lot to do.*
  (We are imposing the obligation on ourselves.)
  Passengers ***must*** *fasten their seat belts.*
  (The obligation is imposed by the airline who wrote the notice.)
  Children ***must*** *wear school uniform at all times when they are in school.*
  You ***mustn't*** *smoke in here.*
  We'll ***have to*** *get there before 5 o'clock because the shops close then.*
  Do you ***have to*** *pay for the tickets in advance?*

- We can also use ***have got to*** to express obligation.
  Have got to is often interchangeable with ***have to*** but there is sometimes a difference.
  Have to can be used for habitual actions and single actions:
  *I **have to** get the bus into work today.*
  *I **have to** get the bus into work every day.*
  Have got to can only be used for single actions:
  *I **have got to** get the bus into work today.*
  (NOT ~~*I have got to get the bus into work every day*~~.)

- To express a negative obligation, use ***mustn't***.
  Do not use ***don't have to***. ***Don't have to*** means there is no obligation:
  *You **mustn't** wait here.* (You are not allowed to wait here.)
  *You **don't have to** wait here.* (It is not necessary for you to wait here but you can if you want to.)

- To express obligation in the past, use ***had to***:
  *I **had to** report the incident to the police.*
  *Did you **have to** get a visa?*

Note: ***Must*** + perfect infinitive is not used to talk about past obligation. It is used to make deductions about the past: *She **must have left** early.*

- To express necessity, use ***need***.
  We can use ***need*** as a modal verb in questions and negative sentences. It is most often used in the negative:
  *You **needn't** come if you don't want to.*
  ***Need** I bring anything with me?*
  We can also use ***need*** as an ordinary verb, followed by the ***to***–infinitive:
  *You **don't need** <u>to come</u> if you don't want to.*
  ***Do** I **need** <u>to bring</u> anything with me?*
  *Everyone **needs** <u>to eat</u> fresh fruit and vegetables.*
  *I'll **need** <u>to buy</u> some new clothes if I get that job.*

- To express lack of necessity in the past, use ***needn't*** + perfect infinitive or ***didn't need to/didn't have to*** + infinitive. There is some difference between them:
  *I **needn't** <u>have gone</u> to the station so early. The train was nearly an hour late.* (It wasn't necessary to go to the station early but I didn't realise that and so I did get there early.)
  *We **didn't need to/didn't have to** <u>get up</u> early this morning because we had no lectures.* (It wasn't necessary and so we didn't do it.)

Note: We do not use ***need*** + perfect infinitive in the positive.

Practice

36 Complete the sentences using the modals ***should***, ***ought to***, ***must***, ***need*** or the verb ***have to*** in the correct tense and form. Put the infinitive into the appropriate form.

1 We ..*had to leave*.. (leave) at 11 o'clock last night because the last bus went at 11.20.

2 I don't think you ..*should / ought to offer*.. (offer) to help him. You've got enough work to do yourself.

3 They .... (not pay) to stay in a hotel. They can stay with us.

4 We've been staying in a hotel for the last two weeks so we .... (not cook) our own meals.

5 You .... (come round) for dinner one evening. We haven't had a good talk for a long time.

6 We .... (run) all the way to the station because we were late for the train.

7 It's your own fault that you're so tired. You .... (not go) to bed so late.

8 Why .... the prisoners .... (be locked) in their cells all day?

9 Hurry up. You .... (not have) a bath now. The taxi's coming in twenty minutes.

10 You .... (not tell) him what happened. He would never forgive us.

11 You .... (not allow) Max to walk home from school every day on his own. He's too young.

12 I don't like .... (do) everything my boss tells me to do.

13 You .... (go) to that new French restaurant in town. It's the best restaurant I've ever been to.

14 Tom .... (not get up) early in the morning but everyone else in the house does.

15 If I fail any one of my exams, I .... (take) all of them again in November.

16 You .... (work) when I came into the room, not talking.

17 I .... (tell) him what you really think of him next time you see him if I were you.

18 The wedding's been cancelled so I .... (not buy) that new suit: it was a waste of money.

19 I .... (take) the children to school every morning before I go to work.

20 You .... (not eat) in the lecture halls: it's against the college regulations.

21 I'd like you to come to the meeting but you .... (not come) if you don't want to.

22 This letter .... (be hidden) where no-one will ever find it. Its contents .... (remain) a secret for ever.

23 .... (you/wear) a uniform at work?

24 Please don't say any more. I already know the truth so you .... (not lie to me).

25 Employees .... (follow) the safety regulations.

37 Offers, requests, permission, suggestions: *can, could, may, might, would, must, shall, would you mind*

- To ask permission or make a request, use:

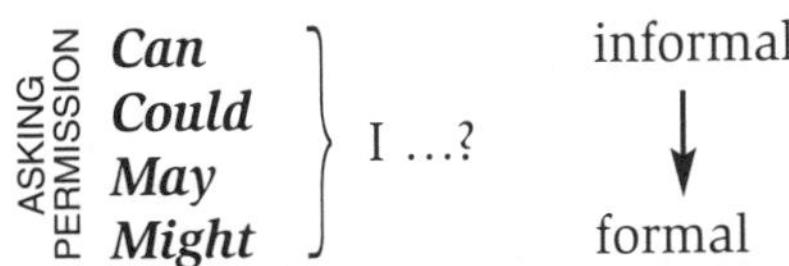

*'**Can** I borrow your pen, please?' 'Yes, of course you **can**.'*
*'Do you think I **could** leave my bag here?' 'Yes, certainly.'*
*'**May** I use your phone, please?' 'Yes, of course you **may**.'*

MAKING A REQUEST
Can / ***Could*** / ***Would*** } you ... ?

*'**Could** you open the door for me, please?' 'Yes, of course.'*

Would you mind + | gerund ...?
| ***if I*** + verb in present or past ...?

*'**Would you mind** | opening the window?' | 'No, of course not.'*
*| **if I** open/opened the window?' |*

- To give or refuse permission, use:
You can/can't/may/may not/must/mustn't ...:

*You **can** stay here if you want to.*
*You **may** borrow these books whenever you like.*
*You **can** go out but you must be back by midnight.*
*I'm afraid you **can't** wait in here.*

These modals can also be used to give permission or make prohibitions in the third person, e.g. in written rules:
*Each player **may** look at the cards once.*
*Candidates **must not** start writing until the examiner tells them to.*

- To make an offer, use:
Can/Shall I, we ...? Would you like ...?
I'll ..., (shall I?), May I ...? (more formal)
***Can** I help you?*
***Shall** I carry that for you?*
***Would you like** some tea?*
***Would you like** me to help you?*
I'll** make you some breakfast, **shall I?
***May** I take your coat?*

- To make a suggestion or an invitation, use:
Shall we ...?, We could ... ., Would you like to ...?:
*'**Shall we** go out for a meal tonight?' 'Yes, that would be nice.'*
*'**We could** have a game of tennis this afternoon.' 'Yes, OK, why not?'*
*'**Would you like to** come round tomorrow?' 'Yes, I would.'*

Practice

37 Write what to say using ***can, could, may, might, shall, must, would, would you like, would you mind***. There may be several possible answers.

1 Offer to open the door for a stranger.
Shall I open the door for you?

2 Ask someone to answer the phone for you.
Would you answer the phone for me, please?

3 Invite a friend to go for a swim this morning.

....

4 Offer to make someone a sandwich.

....

5 Request an appointment to see your bank manager, Ms Arnold.

....

....

6 Give someone permission to use your phone.

....

7 Suggest going for a picnic this afternoon.

....

8 Ask someone to wait here for you.

....

9 Give your son permission to go out but tell him to be back before dark.

....

....

10 You are in a train. Ask another passenger if you can open the window.

....

11 You are the teacher. Give your students permission to work outside today but tell them not to talk too much.

....

....

12 Offer to answer the phone.

....

13 Ask a friend for a pen.

....

38 Habit

would and *used to*

- ***used to*** is not a modal. It is formed like this:
  I ***used to*** *work there.*
  I ***didn't use to*** *work there.*
  Did *you* ***use to*** *work there?*
- Use ***would*** and ***used to*** to talk about past habits:
  When we were children, my brother and I ***used to*** *fight all the time.*
  When we were children, my brother and I ***would*** *fight all the time.*
- When we use ***would*** to talk about a past habit, it is necessary to use a past time reference. ***Used to*** can be used with or without a past time reference.
  I ***used*** *to go out a lot.*
  (NOT ~~*I would go out a lot*~~.)
  Before I got this job, I ***used to/would*** *go out a lot.*
- When we talk about past situations (not actions), we can use ***used to*** but we can't use ***would***:
  We ***used to*** *live in a flat in the town centre.*
  (NOT ~~*We would live in a flat in the town centre*~~).
  She ***used to*** *have long hair but now she wears it short.*

Practice

38 Complete the sentences with ***would*** or ***used to***. Where either form is possible, write them both. Where there is a word in brackets, put it in the correct position.

1 I ..used to.. have lots of free time before I started working here.

2 In the long summer holidays, we ..used to/would.. go out somewhere with a picnic every day.

3 When I was a newly-trained teacher, I .... work till late every night preparing lessons.

4 They .... be happy together but they're not now.

5 When they came to London, they .... (never) travel anywhere on the tube.

6 When I had a car, I .... drive everywhere, but now I'm much fitter because I always walk or cycle.

7 During my last year at university, I .... go to the library to start work at 9 o'clock every morning.

8 When we shared a flat together, we .... (often) stay up talking late into the night.

9 When Amy was a baby, people .... (often) come up to me and tell me how beautiful she was.

10 He .... be very overweight but he's much slimmer now.

11 When I was at school, I .... (never) do my weekend homework until Sunday evening.

12 I .... work in the same department as your sister.

13 When I was a teenager, I .... (often) spend the whole evening just listening to music.

14 She .... have a lot of boyfriends when she was younger.

15 He .... go for a run every day.

Gerunds and infinitives

39 Gerunds and infinitives: uses

The gerund

USES

- Subject of a verb:
  Smoking *is bad for you.*
- Object of a verb:
  Do you like ***cooking****?*
- The complement of ***to be***:
  His favourite activity is ***watching*** *television.*
- After prepositions:
  She's very good at ***listening*** *to people.*
- After determiners (***a***, ***the***, ***this***, ***some***, ***a lot of***):
  The ***bombing*** *of civilians horrified everyone.*
- After possessive adjectives, object pronouns or nouns:
  I hope you don't mind his/him/John ***coming*** *here.*
- After adjectives:
  Regular ***swimming*** *is very good for you.*
  It was awful ***working*** *there.*
- In certain expressions:
  It's no use ***trying*** *to help her.*
  Is this for ***peeling*** *vegetables?*
  How about ***going out*** *for a meal tonight?*
  There are some jobs I hate, like ***washing*** *and* ***ironing*** *the clothes.*
  We usually go ***fishing*** *at the weekend.*
  No ***smoking***

Notes

- Gerunds can take objects and can be qualified by adverbs.
  I enjoy ***reading*** *new books.*
  gerund object

  You should stop ***working*** *so hard.*
  gerund adverb
- The negative gerund form is ***not*** + gerund:
  It's nice ***not being*** *at work.*

The infinitive

USES

- After certain verbs:
  They agreed ***to come****.*
- After certain verbs + person (object):
  I asked her ***to come*** *here.*

- After ***to be***:
  My first thought was ***to phone*** *you.*

- To express purpose:
  I came here ***to tell*** *you the good news.*

- After ***be*** + adjective (+ ***of*** + noun/pronoun):
  It was nice ***to see*** *you.*
  It's kind of you ***to help*** *me.*
  She's very keen ***to do*** *the course.*

- After ***the first/second/last/only/best*** (and other superlative adjectives) + noun or pronoun '***one***':
  He was the only one ***to die***.

- After a noun/pronoun. The verb in the infinitive relates to the preceding noun/pronoun:
  There's a lot of work ***to do***.
  I've got a few people ***to see***.

- After verbs of knowing and believing:
  verb + object + infinitive
  or
  verb in the passive + infinitive
  I know him ***to be*** *an honest man.*
  He is known ***to be*** *an honest man.*
  We consider it ***to be*** *our duty.*
  It is considered ***to be*** *our duty.*

- After verb + question word:
  I don't know what ***to do***.

- After ***too*** + adjective and after adjective + ***enough***:
  He's too ill ***to come***.
  The garden isn't big enough ***to play*** *games in.*

- After ***is/are*** to describe a future event:
  He is ***to become*** *Mayor next month.*

Notes

- Infinitives can take objects and can be qualified by adverbs:
  He expects ***to win*** *the race easily.*
  infinitive object adverb

- The negative infinitive form is ***not*** + (***to***-) infinitive:
  He agreed ***not to tell*** *anyone.*

Verb + infinitive, verb + gerund

The ***to***-infinitive after a verb often describes a future event, an event following the main verb. For example, after ***hope***, ***expect***, ***promise***, ***want***, the event in the ***to***-infinitive comes after the activity or thought in the main verb:
I hope ***to see*** *you next week.*

The gerund describes an activity. It does not indicate a time sequence:
We enjoyed ***seeing*** *you last weekend.*

Practice

39a In your notebook, copy the table and put the following verbs into the correct columns.

~~apologize~~, ~~arrange~~, ~~avoid~~, approve, decide, demand, discourage, dream, enjoy, enquire, expect, finish, help, hope, imagine, insist, intend, invite, learn, would like, look forward, manage, mind, miss, object, offer, plan, pretend, refuse, seem, succeed, want, wish

Verb (+ person) + infinitive	*Verb + preposition + gerund*	*Verb + gerund*
arrange (for s.o.)	*apologize for*	*avoid*

39b Put the verbs in brackets into the infinitive or the gerund.

1 He has promised *to deliver* (deliver) it to me this afternoon.
2 I've invited Mark and Anna .... (stay) for the weekend.
3 I don't mind .... (stay) at home to look after the children.
4 Has she decided .... (take) that job?
5 He's always complaining about .... (work) too hard.
6 He claims .... (be) her brother but I think he's lying.
7 Why are you blaming me for .... (get) lost? You've got the map.
8 We don't believe in .... (buy) each other big presents.
9 I know you don't approve of .... (smoke) so I won't smoke in here.
10 The doctor told me .... (stay) in bed but it's so boring.
11 Don't keep on .... (talk) about it. It's upsetting me.
12 It's raining outside. Would you prefer .... (stay in)?
13 My boss told me .... (not leave) the office before five.

14 It's very nice here but I miss .... (see) my friends.

15 I don't recommend .... (study) on your own.

16 I've always dreamed of .... (live) in a cottage in the country.

17 Sometimes I think you enjoy .... (upset) me.

18 I regret .... (not keep) in touch with my old friends.

19 I'm not expecting him .... (phone) me tonight but I hope he does.

20 Don't forget .... (lock up) when you go to bed.

40 The bare infinitive

We generally use ***to*** with the infinitive, e.g. *I want* ***to see*** *you*. However, in some cases, we use the bare infinitive: that is, the infinitive without ***to***.

USES

- After modals and after the auxiliaries ***do/did***:
  You must ***come****.*
  They may ***arrive*** *soon.*
  Did you ***pass*** *the exam?*
- After ***Let's*** ...:
  [us]
  Let's ***go*** *out tonight.*
- After ***make*** + noun/pronoun object:
  He made me ***come*** *here.*
- After ***would rather***:
  I'd rather ***walk*** *there than take the bus.*
  I'd rather ***not stay*** *out late tonight.*
- After ***had better***:
  We'd better ***go*** *home now.*
- After ***Why not ...?***:
  Why not ***phone*** *me tomorrow?*

- After the verb ***help***, we can use the ***to***–infinitive or the bare infinitive:
  *Can you help me (****to****)* ***open*** *this?*

- After a verb of perception (*see, watch, notice, feel, hear*) + object:
  I didn't hear you ***come in****.*

Note: Present participles also come after verbs of perception. See page 116.

- When there is a series of infinitives after a verb:
  I'd like to come and ***see*** *you.*

Practice

40 In your notebook, copy the dialogue underlining all the infinitives and adding ***to*** where it is required.

Two friends, Alex and Megan, are talking.

A: Megan, where were you last night? I tried *to find* you but I couldn't *see* you anywhere. James says he didn't see you come in to the party.
M: Yes Alex, that's right. I'm sorry. My parents wouldn't let me come out last night. I wanted see you – honestly I did.
A: Why did your parents make you stay in? They usually allow you go out in the evenings, don't they?
M: Yes, but I hadn't finished doing my homework. And they refused let me go out until I had.
A: Oh dear, poor you. Oh well, never mind. Let's do something tonight instead.
M: OK. Actually, I'd like see that new film.
A: Would you? I suppose it might be quite good but I'd rather just go out to the café. I was hoping have a chance talk to you properly.
M: Well, why not do both? We could go to the early showing of the film and then go to the café.
A: I'm not sure I can afford go to the cinema.
M: That's all right. I've got some money.
A: So what time would you like meet, then?
M: Six o'clock I suppose – in the cinema. I'll try get there a bit earlier and buy the tickets.

41 Verbs of perception + object + *ing* or the bare infinitive

Verbs of perception (***see***, ***notice***, ***look at***, ***watch***, ***feel***, ***hear***, ***listen to***) can be followed by the ***ing*** form or the bare infinitive. The verb ***smell*** can only be followed by the ***ing*** form:
The use of the bare infinitive describes the complete action:
I watched her ***play*** *tennis.* (I saw the whole game.)

The use of the ***ing*** form describes the action in progress:
I watched her ***playing*** *tennis.* (I saw the game in progress.)

The ***ing*** form after a verb of perception is a present participle. Verb of perception + present participle is more common than verb of perception + bare infinitive. The difference between the use of the present participle and the use of the bare infinitive is often very small:
I always hear the birds ***singing*** *in the mornings.*
I always hear the birds ***sing*** *in the mornings.*

Note: We use a few other verbs with the present participle: ***find***, ***discover***, ***catch***, ***leave***, ***keep***. These verbs cannot be followed by the bare infinitive:
I <u>found</u> her ***looking*** *in my desk.*

Practice

41 Rewrite the following pairs of sentences as one sentence, using the ***ing*** form or a bare infinitive.

1 I saw you the other day. You were cycling to work.
I saw you cycling to work the other day.

2 I heard him early this morning. He left the house.
I heard him leave the house early this morning.

3 She stood there and watched him. He drove away.
....

4 Did you notice me? I was crying.
....

5 I've often seen you. You've been walking along the beach with your dog.
....
....

6 Have you ever heard him? He plays the saxophone.
....

7 I expect to find you when I get back. You'll be working hard.
....
....

8 Did you hear me? I arrived.
....

9 I looked at the child and felt very sad. She was smiling up at me.

....

....

10 We heard them. They were arguing all night.

....

11 I can feel my hands. They're shaking.

....

12 I watched you and then I left. You went to sleep.

....

13 I never really noticed your hair. It was going grey.

....

14 I can smell smoke. It's coming in through the windows.

....

15 He watches me every weekend. I play football.

....

42 Verbs followed by the *to*–infinitive or the gerund

Some verbs can be followed by the ***to***–infinitive or the gerund, with some change in meaning.

BE
*My favourite watersport **is wind-surfing**.*
(The gerund behaves like a noun and describes an activity.)
*Our plan **is to close** the factory down next year.*
(The ***to***–infinitive describes a complete event. It often describes a future event and is frequently used after words like *plan, aim, intention, decision, solution.*)

REMEMBER
*I **remembered to give** her the message.*
(I remembered first and then I gave her the message.)
*I **remember giving** her the message.*
(I gave her the message and now I remember that I did that.)

FORGET
*I **forgot to go** to that meeting.*
(I forgot and so I didn't go.)
*I **forget going** to that meeting.*
(I forget now that I went.)

TRY
*I **tried to open** the door but it was locked.*
(I tried to do it, but I couldn't. The attempt failed.)
*I couldn't open the door so I **tried using** a different key.*
(***Try doing something*** suggests an experiment. I experimented with using a different key. The result may have been a success or a failure.)

REGRET
*I **regret to say** that your interview was not successful.*
(*I am sorry to say …* . ***Regret*** is quite formal here.)
*I really **regret being** so rude to her.*
(The speaker looks back to an action that took place in the past. The regretting takes place now.)

STOP
*We **stopped to have** a cup of tea.*
(The ***to***-infinitive describes purpose. It introduces the reason why we stopped.)
*We **stopped talking** when she came in.*
(Talking is what we were doing. That is what we stopped doing.)

GO ON
*After an unsuccessful first year at university, he **went on to get** a first-class degree.*
(***go on*** + ***to***-infinitive = move to something different.)
*We **went on talking** all night.*
(***go on*** + gerund = continue doing the same thing)

LIKE / DISLIKE / LOVE / HATE
*I **like going** for a run before work.*
(I enjoy the activity of going for a run before work. I may or may not do it regularly.)
*I **like to go** for a run before work.*
(Describes a regular activity. I like it because I think it's a good idea. I may or may not enjoy the activity while I am actually doing it.)

PREFER
*I don't go out much. I **prefer to stay** at home in the evenings.*
*I don't go out much. I **prefer staying** at home in the evenings.*
(The meaning of these two sentences is very similar.)
*I **prefer staying in** to **going out**.*
(We cannot say: ~~*I prefer to stay in to go out*~~.)
***I'd prefer to stay in** tonight.*
(***Would prefer*** is followed by the infinitive and refers to a specific occasion. NOT ~~***I'd prefer staying in***~~ tonight.)

BEGIN / START / CONTINUE
*He **began/started/continued shouting**.*
*He **began/started/continued to shout**.*
(The meaning of these two sentences is very similar.)

ADVISE / ALLOW / ENCOURAGE / FORBID / RECOMMEND
*They **advised** us **to leave**.*
*They **advised leaving**.*
(These verbs are usually followed by an object [name of a person or a personal pronoun] + ***to***-infinitive. Occasionally they have no object. In that case, they take a gerund.)

NEED
*I **need to get up** early tomorrow.*
(It is necessary for me to do it.)
*The car **needs cleaning**.*
(***Need*** + gerund has a passive meaning. Someone needs to clean the car: it doesn't matter who does it.)

Practice

42 Complete the following texts putting the verbs into the gerund or the ***to***–infinitive.

1 Caroline and Simone, two friends, are talking.

C: Would you like [1] to go out (go out) for a meal tonight?

S: Yes, that would be nice. I just need [2]...................... (wash) my hair first.

C: Shall we go to Perry's?

S: I'd prefer [3]...................... (go) somewhere else. Don't you remember [4]...................... (send) the food back last time we went there? It was terrible.

C: Oh yes, I'd forgotten. We decided to stop [5]...................... (go) there, didn't we?

S: Yes, we did. So I've got another suggestion. Sally recommended [6]...................... (try) that new French restaurant, Chez Victor. She said it was very good. We'll go there, shall we?

C: OK. That's a good idea.

2

Dear Ms Walters,

Thank you for your application for the diploma in tourism but I regret [7]........................... (inform) you that this course is now full. Should you wish to take the course elsewhere, I would advise you [8]........................... (apply) to Central College. They started [9]........................... (run) a course in tourism a year ago and I would recommend you [10]........................... (consider) [11]........................... (enrol) on that course rather than [12]........................... (wait) another year to do a course here. If you would prefer [13]........................... (wait) for this course, then I would encourage you [14]........................... (try) [15]........................... (find) some work related to tourism so that you can start [16]........................... (acquire) some relevant experience.

3 Gareth and Vincent, two friends, are talking.

G: Did you remember [17]...................... (book) the tickets for that concert?

V: Yes, I did, but the problem now is [18]...................... (get) there. My mother says I'm not allowed [19]...................... (borrow) the car this weekend, so I don't know what to do. What about your old motorbike?

G: No, I'm afraid it needs [20]...................... (repair). I could try [21]...................... (ask) my brother if we can have his car. You never know – he might agree.

V: I doubt it. And the tickets were so expensive. I regret [22]...................... (buy) them now. I'm sure we've just wasted the money.

G: I'm sure we haven't. We just need [23]...................... (give) the problem some thought.

V: Actually, I remember [24]...................... (walk) there one night. Mind you, it took about two hours, and we did get a lift home.

G: OK, so we could walk if necessary. Just stop [25]...................... (worry) and start [26]...................... (think).

43 Preposition + gerund

- After prepositions, we use the gerund.
  Preposition + gerund:
  After reading *the letter, he changed his mind.*
  You shouldn't have gone there ***without telling*** *me.*

  Adjective/noun + preposition + gerund:
  Are you ***interested in applying*** *for this job?*
  He's expressed a lot of ***interest in applying*** *for this job.*

  Verb + preposition + gerund/phrasal verb + gerund:
  They ***succeeded in getting*** *the new contract.*
  She ***apologized for upsetting*** *him.*
  They ***carried on working****.*

  Verb + object (person/personal pronoun) + preposition + gerund:
  We ***dissuaded him from writing*** *the letter.*
  She ***accused me of cheating****.*

  Verb + preposition + object pronoun or possessive adjective + gerund:
  My boss ***complained about me/my arriving*** *late last week.*
  They ***agreed on us/our sharing*** *the expenses.*
  Also: ***What about me/my coming*** *to see you tomorrow?*

Note: We use an object pronoun (**me**, **us**) more often than a possessive adjective (**my**, **our**) after a preposition. The use of a possessive adjective is rather formal.

Note: to may be part of the ***to***-infinitive or it may be a preposition preceding a gerund:
We're hoping ***to see*** *you this weekend.*
We're looking forward to ***seeing*** *you this weekend.*

Practice

43a Complete the sentences with the correct preposition and the gerund.

1 Don't try and discourage me ...from doing... (do) what I want to do.
2 I'd like to enquire .... (enrol) on one of your evening courses.
3 She seems very excited .... (start) that new job.
4 Are you thinking .... (leave) him?
5 I think we're all in agreement .... (cut) our costs.
6 She lives on her own but she relies .... the neighbours .... (help) her.
7 She insisted .... (pay) the bill.
8 I expect he's very depressed .... (lose) his job.
9 I think you should apologize .... (not tell) me the truth.
10 I've never approved .... young people .... (stay out) late.
11 Stop talking and get on .... (write) your essays.
12 Why do you always blame me .... (start) the arguments?
13 It's lovely here. It's a great improvement .... (live) in that awful flat.
14 I warned them .... (buy) that car.
15 They're planning .... (expand) the company.

43b Complete the sentences with the infinitive or the gerund.

1 She's hoping to ...finish... (finish) writing her thesis soon.
2 Are you looking forward to ...seeing... (see) James again?
3 The Government are opposed to .... (spend) more money on public transport.
4 I've been waiting to .... (see) you for ages.
5 Alison has persuaded me not to .... (do) it.
6 It's very difficult for him because he's not used to .... (speak) English.
7 Have you never wanted to .... (get) married?

8 In addition to .... (work) such long hours, she also does all the jobs in the house.

9 I've been thinking about it all night, but I'm no closer to .... (find) a solution.

10 It was very unfortunate that you forgot to .... (post) that letter.

11 The key to .... (sleep) soundly is to have regular exercise.

12 I don't know why you object to .... (work) with her. She seems very nice.

13 When did you decide to .... (give up) the course?

14 This problem is similar to .... (have) problems with money: it's not a problem until you find you haven't got any.

15 They're proposing to .... (open) a new airport just outside the town.

44 *be* + adjective + infinitive

- ***be*** + adjective + ***to***–infinitive:
  The verb in the infinitive often refers to an event in the future:
  *He **is keen to change** his job.*
  *They**'re willing to lend** us the money.*
  *We**'re sure to have** a good time.*

- ***be*** + adjective of feeling + ***to***–infinitive:
  *I**'m pleased to see** you.*
  *We **were sorry to hear** your news.*

- ***be*** + adjective describing personal characteristic + (**of** person) + ***to***–infinitive:
  *It **was silly of her to say** that.*
  *It**'s good of you to come**.*
  *It **was selfish of me to ignore** you.*

- ***be*** + adjective describing the activity + ***to***–infinitive:
  *This book **is** very **difficult to read**.*
  *She**'s** very **amusing to talk** to.*

Note: After adjectives like *nice, lovely, great, wonderful, awful* and *horrible,* we can use the ***ing*** form (present participle) or the ***to***–infinitive:
*It's **nice seeing** you.*
*It's **nice to see** you.*
The ***ing*** form describes the activity in progress and the ***to***–infinitive describes the whole event. But in practice, the use of the two forms is very similar.

Practice

44 Rewrite the sentences using ***be*** + adjective + ***to***–infinitive.

1 We're going to leave. We're ready.
We're ready to leave.

2 He's afraid of telling her the truth.
....

3 I received your letter. I was delighted.
....

4 I heard about their divorce. I was surprised.
....

5 You shouldn't interrupt people. It's rude.
....

6 You brought those flowers. It was very kind of you.
....

7 Heating this house is very expensive.
....

8 I saw you last night. It was lovely.
....

9 Having interests outside work is important.
....

10 That child learns very quickly.
....

45 The infinitive and gerund: mixed uses

Before doing the next exercise, re-read the list of uses on pages 111-113.

Practice

45 Put the verbs in the dialogue into the ***to***–infinitive or the gerund.

Helen has been called to the office of her boss, Andrea.

A: Take a seat, Helen. Would you like [1]..*to have*.. (have) some coffee?

H: Er, no thank you.

A: I asked [2]................................... (see) you [3]................................... (talk) about your work. I think there are a few things that we need [4]................................... (discuss).

H: Oh dear. Is there some problem? I do love [5]................................... (work) here and I think I'm getting better at [6]................................... (do) the job.

A: Yes, I'm sure you are, Helen, but sometimes you are rather slow [7]................................... (learn). In a hotel of this reputation, we cannot afford [8]................................... (make) mistakes and I am sorry [9]................................... (say) that you have made rather a lot. There are some things you are very good at, like [10]................................... (welcome) the guests, [11]................................... (talk) to them and [12]................................... (give) them any help they require.

H: That's true. I was rather shy when I first started [13]................................... (work) here but now I'm much better at [14]...................................

(communicate) with the guests. They have often said to me that it is nice [15]................................... (see) such a friendly face at reception.

A: That's good. It's true [16]................................... (say) that you have got much better at [17]................................... (deal) with people. But you do not pay enough attention to [18]................................... (ensure) that the administrative part of your job is carried out efficiently.

H: [19]................................... (Keep) the records is not my favourite part of the job, I must admit.

A: But it's essential [20]................................... (do) that properly. It's no use [21]................................... (be) nice to all the guests if you are creating problems for them by [22]................................... (fail) [23]................................... (carry out) your job efficiently. I know there is a lot of work [24]................................... (do) at reception, but last week you made three mistakes with the billing. That's not good enough.

H: Yes, I'm sorry about that, but sometimes the bills are very complicated [25]................................... (work out).

A: I know, but we can't make mistakes and that's that. And what about you [26]................................... (accept) that booking for the penthouse suite at the weekend when we were using it for a conference? It was very careless of you [27]................................... (do) that. I had to do a lot of [28]................................... (apologize) [29]................................... (calm down) those guests. They were furious.

H: Yes, it was terrible. I do try [30]................................... (get) everything right but I can't help [31]................................... (make) mistakes sometimes. I just don't know what [32]................................... (do) about it.

A: Well, I do. You've got a month [33]................................... (prove) to me that you can do the job efficiently, and if you can't, you'll have [34]................................... (start) [35]................................... (look) for another job.

46 Different forms of the gerund and the infinitive

The gerund and the infinitive can be used in the following forms:

Gerund

gerund	*doing*
perfect gerund	*having done*
passive gerund	*being done*
perfect passive gerund	*having been done*

Infinitive

infinitive	*(to) do*
continuous infinitive	*(to) be doing*
perfect infinitive	*(to) have done*
perfect continuous infinitive	*(to) have been doing*
passive infinitive	*(to) be done*
perfect passive infinitive	*(to) have been done*

Practice

46 Complete the sentences with the appropriate form of the gerund or the infinitive.

1 His greatest ambition is ..*to be chosen*.. (choose) to take part in the Olympics.

2 .... (accept) for that course changed my life.

3 Please come in. I'm sorry .... (keep) you waiting.

4 It is understood that the escaped prisoner might .... (hide) in a friend's house for the last month.

5 I saw Amy last night. She seems .... (get) much better.

6 He denied .... (say) it to me.

7 We congratulated him on .... (get) the job.

8 I hope .... (live) in my own house in five years' time.

9 The children are looking forward to .... (film) for that television programme.

10 I'm sorry I wasn't in when you came round. I would like .... (see) you.

11 I can't see Tony. He seems .... (leave).

12 He denied .... (take part) in the robbery.

13 He is suspected of .... (lie) in order to get the job.

14 The Director is understood .... (resign) last week because of the impending fraud investigation.

15 I hate .... (ask) my age.

16 The builders are expecting .... (finish) the job by the time we get back.

17 He was a difficult child, probably due to .... (look after) by a series of different foster parents.

18 She can't .... (dance) with Tim last night. He's got a broken leg.

19 She seems .... (lose) a lot of weight recently, but otherwise I think she's all right.

20 He doesn't respond very well to .... (ask) to do things.

Reported speech

47 Reported statements

In reported speech (also known as indirect speech), the tense used in the speaker's original words is usually (but not always) moved back a tense when the reporting verb (*said, told*, etc.) is in the past. The tense does not change if the reporting verb is in the present, present perfect or future.

Tense changes

Speaker's words		*Reported speech*
present simple	→	past simple
present continuous	→	past continuous
present perfect simple	→	past perfect simple
present perfect continuous	→	past perfect continuous
past simple	→	past perfect simple
past continuous	→	past perfect continuous
past perfect	→	past perfect
going to future	→	*was going to*
shall/will	→	*would*
shall in offers and suggestions	→	*should*
must	→	*had to*
can	→	*could*

Example: *'Sales **have dropped** dramatically in the last year.'*
*A representative said (that) sales **had dropped** dramatically in the last (or previous) year.*

Note: It is possible to omit ***that***.

When the tense doesn't change

The past simple and continuous often remain unchanged in reported speech, in both written and spoken English, if this can be done without causing any confusion about the time of the actions.
It is also possible for other tenses to remain unchanged in reported speech in spoken English.

Past continuous

- The past continuous usually remains unchanged in reported speech:
  *'When they arrived, I **was** still **cooking** the dinner.'*
  *He said that when they arrived, he **was** still **cooking** the dinner.*

*'I **was working** until ten o'clock last night.'*
*She said that she **was working** until ten o'clock last night/the previous night.*

- Where the past continuous is used to refer to an activity that was completed before an event in the past simple or present perfect, we are more likely to change the past continuous to the past perfect continuous:
*'We **were planning** to go out but then Joe started feeling sick.'*
*She said that they **had been planning** to go out but then Joe started/had started feeling sick.*

Past simple

- When the past simple is used in a time clause, it does not generally change. When there is a time clause, the verb in the main clause can remain in the past simple or change to the past perfect:
*'When I **got** there the place **was** almost empty.'*
*She said that when she **got** there, the place **was/had been** almost empty.*
- When the past simple is used to refer to a situation that still exists in the present, it does not generally change:
*'We didn't stay in the hotel because it **was** too expensive.'*
(And presumably the hotel is still expensive now.)
*She said that they hadn't stayed in the hotel because it **was** too expensive.*
- In other circumstances it is better to change the past simple to the past perfect in written reporting. However, in oral reporting, it is becoming increasingly common to leave the past simple unchanged:
*'I **enjoyed** myself last night.'*
Oral reporting: *Clare said that she **enjoyed** (had enjoyed) herself last night/on Saturday night.*
Written reporting: *Clare said that she **had enjoyed** herself last night/the previous night/on Saturday night.*

Present tenses

- In oral reporting, it is becoming increasingly common not to change the present tenses if the activity is still going on or the situation still exists at the time of reporting:
*'Alison**'s living** with her parents now.'*
*Jo told me that Alison **is living** (was living) with her parents now.*

  *'I can't come to the party because I**'m doing** my homework.'*
  *He said that he can't (couldn't) come to the party because he **was doing** his homework.*

  However, if the party is now finished and he is no longer doing his homework, then we change the tense in reported speech:
  *He said that he couldn't come to the party because he **was doing** his homework.*

  - *'The school **takes on** new students every month.'*

  Assuming that this situation still exists, the verb can stay in the present simple or change to the past simple in oral reporting:
  *The receptionist told me that the school **takes on/took on** new students every month.*

The future

In oral reporting, the future tenses can remain unchanged if the event is still in the future:
*'I'**m meeting** John tonight.'*
*Sheila said that she **is meeting/was meeting** John tonight.*
(Tonight is still in the future.)
BUT
*Sheila said that she **was meeting** John last night.*
(Tonight is now in the past.)

*'We'**re going to launch** a thorough investigation.'*
*The police said that they **are going to/were going to launch** a thorough investigation.*

*'There **will be** no increase in taxes.'*
*The Prime Minister said that there **will/would** be no increase in taxes.*

*'The plane **will be leaving** in thirty-five minutes.'*
*They announced that the plane **will/would be leaving** in thirty-five minutes.*

Time and place changes

It is often necessary to change time, place and other references in reported speech, depending on when and where the reporting takes place in relation to the actual words.

Some common changes

now	→	then
tonight	→	that night
yesterday	→	the day before/on + name of day
tomorrow	→	the following day/the next day/on + name of day
this morning	→	that morning
last week	→	the previous week
next Saturday	→	the following Saturday
ago	→	before/previously
here	→	there
this + the place	→	that/the + the place
this	→	that/the

Note: In the following exercises, you should make the tense changes as for written reporting.

Practice

47 In your notebook, rewrite the sentences in reported speech.

1 'I'll come and see you on Friday if that's all right.' (She said)
She said (that) she would come and see us on Friday if that was all right.
2 'The conference will be spending a considerable time discussing the world debt crisis.' (The statement said)
3 'The shop's closing in half an hour.' (She explained)
4 'He's planning to set up his own business.' (Gareth tells me)
5 'We're going to have to make quite a few cutbacks.' (The managing director said)
6 'The police have been investigating new allegations of fraud.' (A spokesperson said)
7 'When the project first started, there was a lot of interest in it.' (She explained)
8 'It's pouring with rain down here.' (She told me)
9 'I'll have finished writing the report by the time you get here.' (She promised me)
10 'My new computer has made a lot of difference to me.' (She says)
11 'The 8.45 train from Waterloo will be arriving in approximately five minutes.' (The station announcer has just said)
12 'When we were setting up the organisation, we had very little money.' (They told me)
13 'The club lost quite a lot of money last month.' (The treasurer told the meeting)
14 'It will be a very difficult time for all of us.' (He agreed)
15 'You work too hard. You should take more time off.' (He told me)

48 Reported questions

The rules about tense changes apply to questions in the same way as they apply to statements.

- ***Wh*** questions
  The subject and verb are NOT inverted in reported speech:
  *'Why **didn't you tell** me the truth?'*
  inversion

  *She asked me why **I hadn't told** her the truth.*
  subject + verb

- ***Yes/no*** questions
  Put ***if*** or ***whether*** before the subject + verb:
  *'**Have I seen** you before?'*
  *She asked me **if she had seen** me before.*

to–infinitive in reported speech

- In reported requests, advice, commands, etc., use ***to***–infinitive:
  'Can you help me write my speech?'
  *She asked me **to help** her write her speech.*
  'Don't stay out too late.'
  *She told me **not to stay out** too late.*

- When reporting ***shall/should*** questions, we can use ***to***-infinitive after the question word:
  'How much should we give them?'
  *He wanted to know how much **to give** them.*
  'What should I buy for Peter?'
  *She asked me what **to buy** for Peter.*
  'Should I tell her what happened?'
  *He wanted to know whether **to tell** her what had happened.*

Note: We do not use the ***to***-infinitive after ***why*** or ***if***.

Practice

48 Write the following in reported speech.

1 'Where do you think we should advertise?' (He asked me)
He asked me where I thought we should advertise.

2 'Are you going to audition for the play?' (Emma asked me)
....
....

3 'Give me a ring if you need any help.' (She told me)
....
....

4 'How is Laura getting on?' (She often asks me … you …)
....
....

5 'Shall I ask her out for a meal?' (He's been wondering)
....
....

6 'Why did Matthew look so embarrassed when he saw Carole?' (He asked)
....
....

7 'Must we stay here all evening?' (He asked)
....
....

8 'What are they doing about publicity for the event?' (She wondered)
....
....

9 'Will you send me the report when it's finished?' (He asked me)

10 'What have you done with the student records?' (She asked me)

11 'Do you think you could keep your voices down a bit?' (She asked us)

12 'Where did you buy that hat?' (He wanted to know)

13 'Have you been eating properly?' (The doctor asked me)

14 'Don't make any noise during the performance.' (They asked us)

15 'Were you still teaching music when you met Oliver?' (Mike asked me)

49 Verbs used in reporting

Many different verbs are used in reporting. We do not usually report every word that was said or written and these different verbs can help to summarize the original words:
'Would you like to come and stay for the weekend?'
→ *He **invited** us to stay for the weekend.*

'No, no, I don't want your money. I'm definitely going to pay for the meal and that's that.'
→ *She **insisted** on paying for the meal.*

Examples of verbs used in reporting

advise someone agree decide encourage s.o. invite s.o. offer promise refuse warn s.o. (not to …) remind s.o. persuade s.o.	+ INFINITIVE

accuse s.o. of agree on/about apologize for complain about insist on recommend suggest warn against advise s.o. against dissuade s.o. from persuade s.o. against	+ GERUND

agree complain decide insist recommend suggest (+ should) announce boast claim claim concede	+ *that* clause

Practice

49 Put the sentences into reported speech, summarizing what was said and using the verbs in the box.

decide complain accuse advise apologize ~~offer~~ ~~persuade~~ remind warn refuse

1 'I know you've got a lot of work to do at the moment. I'll help you type up that report if you like,' he said.
He offered to help me type up the report.

2 A: I don't think you should hand in your resignation immediately. Give yourself more time to think about it.
B: OK. I suppose you're right. I'll leave it for a while then.
He persuaded me not to hand in my resignation immediately.

3 'No, I'm not going to discuss it with you. I think it's a waste of time,' he said.
....

4 'I really think I should have been invited to the meeting. I'm very unhappy about the fact that I wasn't,' he said.

....

....

5 'You've been quite ill and you need to recover. I really think you should take it easy for a few days,' the doctor said.

....

....

6 'You must not go near their house again or there will be trouble,' the police said to him.

....

....

7 'After giving the matter some serious thought, we have now reached a final decision. We are going to close down the naval base in two years' time,' said the Ministry of Defence.

....

....

8 'Someone's been reading my diary. I know they have. I found it in the wrong drawer this morning. It was you, wasn't it?'

....

....

9 'Remember that you've got to apply for a new passport. Yours is out of date now,' he said to me.

....

10 'I'm really sorry about all the trouble I've caused. I didn't mean to,' she said.

....

....

50 Summarizing when reporting

When we are reporting, we do not repeat everything that was said or written. As we report, we summarize.

A range of different verbs are used and these help to summarize. (See page 134.)

In addition, we often use adjectives to describe how someone responded, instead of reporting their words:

'Oh, that's fantastic. I'm just so pleased. This is the best news we've had in ages.'
——► *She was* ***delighted*** *when we told her the news.*

Oral reporting

When we report orally, we regularly switch our method of reporting. We use a mixture of direct speech, reported speech and descriptions of the content of the conversation. For example:

I was talking to Jo last night about the holiday. She thinks we shouldn't book anything up yet because we'll probably get a cheaper deal if we leave it till just before we go. I agreed with her but I said I didn't know what you would think about that. And then of course we have to decide definitely where we want to go. I said we quite fancied going to one of the islands but she said, 'Well, I'm not sure Graham will like the idea.' Anyway, in the end she said why don't we talk to him about it when we meet him on Thursday.

Written reporting

In written reports, we tend to use reported speech consistently rather than switching from one style of reporting to another. If we are reporting what one person said, it is not necessary to keep repeating **She/He/It said ...** . However, we continue to use the reported speech tenses if it is understood that we are still reporting. For example:

The meeting was concluded by the Chair of the Governors, who said that although it had been a difficult year, the staff of the school had managed very well. The financial cutbacks had hit hard and it was to be hoped that there would be no further cutbacks in the coming year. Library stocks were severely depleted and he suggested that there should be a series of fundraising activities to help raise money for books. He thanked all the staff for their hard work and hoped that the coming year would be successful. The Headteacher then thanked the Chair of the Governors for his contribution to the school and the meeting was closed at 9.00 p.m.

Practice

50 In your notebook, write a summarized report of the following speech.

'I am delighted to have been elected onto the Council and I thank all those voters who came out in the rain today to vote for me. I am very much looking forward to representing the interests of the residents of Kimbridge Valley and hope that I will have the opportunity to do so for many years to come.

During the last few weeks, I have spoken to many of the valley residents on the doorstep and I have a clear idea of the issues which are of most concern to them. The proposed closure of the school is understandably causing a great deal of anxiety and I shall do everything in my power to fight against that. I hope that I will be successful.

Thanks again to my supporters and a big thank you to all those who helped me during the campaign.'

Example:
In her acceptance speech, Diane Banham said that she was delighted ...

Sentence structure

Introduction

Simple sentences

- Subject + verb:

S	V
The rice	*is burning.*

- Subject + verb + complement:

S	V	COMP.
She	*'s*	*a lawyer.*

S	V	COMP.
She	*'s*	*intelligent.*

- Subject + verb + direct object:

S	V	D.O.
I	*'ve read*	*this book.*

- Subject + verb + indirect object + direct object:

S	V	I.O.	D.O.
My boyfriend	*wrote*	*me*	*a lovely letter.*

- Subject + verb + object + complement:

S	V	O	COMP.
They	*made*	*him*	*a star.*

S	V	O	COMP.
They	*made*	*him*	*very famous.*

Compound sentences

We can link simple sentences to form compound sentences of two or more clauses. In a compound sentence, the clauses are of equal importance. We can make the link in the following ways:

- With a co-ordinating conjunction, e.g. ***and***, ***but***, ***so***, ***yet***, sometimes preceded by a comma:
  He loves her **but** *she doesn't love him.*
- With a semi-colon or colon:
  *I met David yesterday***;** *he's just come out of hospital.*
  or *I met David yesterday***:** *he's just come out of hospital.*
- With a semi-colon or a colon followed by a connecting adverb. e.g. ***however***, ***nevertheless***, ***meanwhile***, ***after all***, ***finally***:
  He performed very well in the interview; ***however***, *he didn't get the job.*
  or *He performed very well in the interview:* ***however***, *he didn't get the job.*

Complex sentences

Complex sentences have a main clause and one or more subordinate clauses or phrases. We can link the clauses as follows:

- With relative clauses:
  Many people ***who are out of work*** *become depressed.*
- With noun clauses:
  I've always known ***that he hated me****.*
- With adverbial clauses:
  Did you see him ***when he came in****?*
- With infinitive or participial constructions:
  To do the job properly*, you'll need to get some tools.*
  She ran out of the house ***calling for help****.*

51 Conjunctions

Common conjunctions

To ***link****:* and, both … and, or, either … or, neither … nor, not only … but (also)
To ***contrast****:* but, however, nevertheless, though/although, in spite of, despite, whereas
To ***express a reason or purpose****:* because, for, as, since, so that, in order that
To ***express a consequence****:* so, therefore
To ***make an additional point****:* besides, moreover, anyway

Practice

51 In your notebook, join the sentences with a suitable conjunction. There may be more than one possible answer for each sentence.

1 I went to bed early. I would be able to get up early.
I went to bed early so that I would be able to get up early.
I went to bed early in order that I would be able to get up early.
2 It's an excellent course. I'm very lucky to get a place on it.
3 I don't really want to go to the cinema tonight. I can't afford it.
4 There is very little that the company can do about this. It is not their responsibility.
5 I've known her for a long time. I don't know much about her private life.
6 She's extremely generous. Her husband is the exact opposite.
7 I didn't say that. I didn't even think it.
8 The suspect is critically ill in hospital. We can't interview him for the time being.
9 I like working here. The people are very friendly.
10 I could do the work tonight. I could get up early in the morning to do it.
11 In a way, I love the job. I hate it.
12 He looks a bit overweight. He is quite fit.
13 The economy has been in recession all year. Our sales have remained steady.
14 I've brought a photograph. You can see how beautiful the place is.
15 The Government are getting worried. They're losing popularity.

16 I had a terrible headache last night. I couldn't go out.
17 My job is very interesting. It doesn't pay very well.
18 You leave now. I'll call the police.

52 Noun clauses

A noun clause is sometimes called a ***that***–clause. However, noun clauses do not always use ***that***.

- Noun clause as object.
  Many verbs can be followed by a noun clause:
  I can guarantee ***(that) it will be there on time****.*
  Do you think ***(that) she'll come****?*

- Noun clause as subject:
  That you don't love him *is obvious.*
  However, we more often use the construction:
  It + ***be/seem*** + adjective + noun clause
  It is obvious ***(that) you don't love him****.*
  or we use: *The fact that …*:
  The fact ***that you don't love him*** *is obvious.*

- Noun clause after certain adjectives, e.g. adjectives describing feelings: *pleased, sorry, happy, glad, delighted, upset, worried, concerned, surprised, grateful*, and adjectives describing degrees of certainty: *sure, positive, convinced, doubtful*:
  I'm concerned ***(that) he won't believe me****.*
  Are you sure ***(that) he said that****?*

- Noun clause after a large number of abstract nouns, e.g. *belief, idea, fact, hope, promise, suggestion, thought, reason, implication, something/anything.*

  As object: *I don't like the suggestion* ***that we do this job together****.*

  As subject: *The thought* ***that I upset her so much*** *is awful.*

- Noun clause with question words.
  Noun clauses that start with a question word do not start with *that*.

  As object: *I will never understand* ***why he did that****.*
  or ***Why he did that*** *I will never understand.*
  I looked at ***what they'd done****.*

  As subject: ***What happened between us*** *must remain a secret.*

- Noun clauses with *if/whether* (*or not*).

  As object:
  I don't know ***if/whether he's coming tonight****.*

  As subject: ***Whether or not he's coming tonight*** *is still uncertain.*
  It is still uncertain ***if/whether/whether or not he's coming tonight****.*

Practice

52a Underline the noun clauses in the following dialogue.

Angie and Helen are talking at work. Angie is Helen's boss.

A: Helen, I'm delighted to hear <u>that you've decided to accept the post of junior manager</u>.
H: Yes. I just hope that it turns out all right.
A: Oh, I'm sure it will. Is there anything in particular that you're worried about?
H: Well, yes. I'm not sure how the staff will respond to me as a manager. After all, I am quite a bit younger than most of them.
A: Oh, I wouldn't worry too much about that. I expect that some of them will be a bit hostile to you at first but they'll soon get used to the fact that you're the boss. It's important that you appear confident in your position, even if you don't feel very confident. The reason that you got this position at your age is that you're good and you must remember that.
H: Well, I hope that I will live up to your expectations of me. I will certainly try.

52b Join the sentences together using a noun clause. Make changes where necessary.

1 He's lying to you. I'm sure.

I'm sure that he's lying to you.

2 You did something. It is unforgivable.

What you did is unforgivable.

It is unforgivable what you did.

3 She still holds on to the belief. He isn't dead.

....

....

4 She hasn't made a complaint. We must be grateful for that.

....

....

5 Some people are coming to the meeting. I don't know how many.

....

....

6 She didn't lie to you about it. That suggestion is ridiculous.

....

....

7 You're going with him. I presume that.

....

8 Judith's coming round tonight. Have you forgotten that?

....

....

9 She may have passed her exams. I don't know.

....

....

10 He didn't tell her the truth. She is very angry about that.

....

....

11 She may be good enough to do the job: she may not. It remains doubtful.

....

....

12 He has some emotional problems. That is quite apparent.

....

....

13 Where are we going to meet tonight? Have you arranged that?

....

....

14 How is she? Do you know?

....

15 They're getting married. I'm delighted.

....

53 Participial constructions: present participial phrases

After verbs

- After verbs of sensation: *see, hear, feel, smell, listen, notice, watch*:
  I saw her ***leaving the house very early this morning****.*

  Note: These verbs can also be followed by a bare infinitive which implies completeness:
  I saw her ***leave*** *the house early this morning.*
  i.e. I saw her whole departure.

- After *catch, find, leave*:
  I caught him ***looking through my drawers****.*

- After *go, come, spend time, waste time, be busy*:
  Would you like to come ***skiing with us****?*

In place of clauses

Participial phrases in place of clauses are quite formal and are used most often in written language.
A participle must have the same subject as the verb in the main clause. We use them:

- when two actions by the same subject take place at the same time:
  She held his hand and led him through the crowd.
  Holding his hand*, she led him through the crowd.*
  She led him through the crowd ***holding his hand****.*

- when one action immediately follows another or is a direct result of it. The main action is a finite verb and the secondary action is a participle. The action which takes place first is written first:
  I stayed at home and watched television.
  I stayed at home ***watching television****.*

  I saw her on the other side of the road and quickly tried to hide.
  Seeing her on the other side of the road*, I quickly tried to hide.*

  She turned on her computer and started work.
  Turning on her computer*, she started work.*

  He told her not to eat it and explained that there was a risk of food poisoning.
  He told her not to eat it, ***explaining that there was a risk of food poisoning****.*

- in place of clauses of time.
  (present or perfect participle after time conjunctions *after, before, since, while, on*)

  clause of time
  After I spoke to you, | *I felt much better.*

  After speaking/having spoken to you*, I felt much better.*
  I felt much better ***after speaking/having spoken to you****.*

  When I first met him, I didn't like him.
  I didn't like him ***on first meeting him****.*

- in place of clauses of reason.
  We use a present participle in place of a clause of reason in the present simple, present continuous, past simple or past continuous:

clause of reason
As/Since/Because I was happy with my results, | *I decided to go out and celebrate.*

Being happy with my results*, I decided to go out and celebrate.*

We use a perfect participle in place of a clause of reason in the present perfect or past perfect:

clause of reason
He's lived here all his life | *so he knows a lot about the town.*

Having lived here all his life*, he knows a lot about the town.*

I'd had an argument with him the night before so I didn't want to see him.
Having had an argument with him the night before*, I didn't want to see him.*

- in place of clauses of concession.
  After *although* and *while*:
  While fully understanding your problem*, I can't allow you to break the rules.*
- In place of defining subject relative clauses in the present simple or continuous:
  The woman who lives/who is living next door works for a television company.
  The woman **living next door** *works for a television company.*

Practice

53 In your notebook, rewrite the sentences below using a present participial or perfect participial phrase.

1 I smelt something. It was burning.
I smelt something burning.
2 I went round to see her. I was hoping for a reconciliation.
3 While he hated the job, he did it for many years.
4 She came in. She looked furious.
5 I had plenty of time to spare so I had a good look round the town.
6 He was wearing only a pair of shorts. He walked out into the darkness.

7 I had been out all day so I was quite happy to stay in for the evening.
8 The bedrooms that overlook the sea are the best ones in the hotel.
9 We're wasting time. We're sitting here and doing nothing.
10 I have changed my job since I last wrote to you.
11 Before I make a decision, I need to discuss it with my partner.
12 We had been friends for twenty years and suddenly we had a big argument and haven't seen each other since.
13 I had failed one of my exams so I couldn't get into university.
14 Because he loved her so much, he forgave her for everything.
15 I left them. They were doing the washing-up.

54 Participial constructions: past participial phrases

The past participle can sometimes replace subject + passive verb in the same way as the present participle can sometimes replace subject + active verb.

- Past participle in place of the passive:
  I often saw her at the disco. She was surrounded by her admirers.
  I often saw her at the disco, ***surrounded by her admirers****.*

  He was loved by all who knew him. He devoted his life to others.
  Loved by all who knew him*, he devoted his life to others.*

  Her books, which are read by people all over the world, are still immensely popular.
  Her books, ***read by people all over the world****, are still immensely popular.*

  Although it was intended to be a nice surprise, the party was not what I wanted at all.
  Although ***intended to be a nice surprise****, the party was not what I wanted at all.*

  If I am accepted for the job, I'll have to start at the beginning of next month.
  If ***accepted for the job****, I'll have to start at the beginning of next month.*

  The manuscript had been lost for many years when it suddenly turned up again.
  Lost for many years*, the manuscript suddenly turned up again.*

- ***Being*** + past participle following *after, before, when, since, while, on, by:*
  After it was cleaned the bike looked as good as new.
  After ***being cleaned****, the bike looked as good as new.*

  Since the government was elected, it has had one crisis after another.
  Since ***being elected****, the government has had one crisis after another.*

  When he was being questioned, he suddenly burst into tears.
  When ***being questioned****, he suddenly burst into tears.*

  The message got across to people because it was repeated over and over again.
  The message got across to people by ***being repeated over and over again****.*

Practice

54 Rewrite the sentences below using a past participial phrase or ***being*** + past participial phrase.

1 I was exhausted through lack of sleep and fell asleep at my desk.
Exhausted through lack of sleep, I fell asleep at my desk.

2 Peter was abandoned by his parents at an early age and took to stealing.

....

....

3 Although it was written many years ago, the book is still relevant today.

....

....

4 Since I was promoted, I've had no time to go out.

....

....

5 The boy was taken from his parents at an early age. He had a very difficult life.

....

....

6 The money was hidden in the cellar. It was not discovered for many years.

....

....

7 He was frequently criticized for his self-centred attitude but was nonetheless very popular.

....

....

8 After he was released from prison, Andy could not find a job anywhere.

....

....

9 The committee meetings, which were always dominated by the same people, were slow-moving and ineffectual.

....

....

10 When he was caught, he confessed everything. (On ...)

....

11 When it is seen from the outside, the building looks a mess, but it is lovely inside.

....

....

12 If we are elected, we will increase the value of pensions.

....

....

13 Although he was ridiculed by everybody, he continued to pursue his bizarre projects.

....

....

14 Unless it is destroyed, this material could have damaging consequences.

....

....

15 Jennifer had been shoplifting for many years before she was found out.

....

....

55 Adverbial clauses of time, place, manner and reason

Adverbial clauses, like adverbs, tell us something further about the verb and answer the questions ***When?***, ***Where?***, ***How?***, ***Why?***, etc.
Here are some of the most common conjunctions used to introduce adverbial clauses:

Time	when, after, before, as, as soon as, by the time (that), once, since, until/till, wherever, while
Place	where, wherever, anywhere, everywhere
Manner	as, as if, as though
Comparison	than, as ... as
Reason	because, as, since
Purpose	so that, in order that, in case
Result	so ... that, such a ... that
Condition	if, unless, provided/providing (that), so/as long as
Contrast	although/though/even though, while, whereas, however, (+ much/good/badly), whatever, whenever, wherever

Note: We generally use the present simple to refer to the future in adverbial clauses of time and condition:
When/If I ***come*** *to London, I'll come and see you.*
and we use the present perfect in place of the future perfect:
*When I****'ve finished*** *my dinner, I'll come and help you.*

Practice

55a Underline the adverbial clauses and complete them with an appropriate conjunction.

In some sentences, more than one conjunction is possible.

1 I'm sorry I wasn't here earlier but I came ...as soon as... I could.

2 I'm staying in all weekend .... I can get my work done.

3 He spoke to me .... it was all my fault.

4 He didn't react .... I'd hoped; he was actually rather angry.

5 Things are never .... bad .... you think they are.

6 You are growing fast. You're taller .... your mother is now.

7 He'd like to be an actor .... his father would like him to be a lawyer.

8 She's .... interested in her work .... she never seems to do anything else.

9 I'll meet you .... you like; I don't mind where it is.

10 I won't believe you .... I've seen it for myself.

11 She seems happy .... she can't find a job.

12 .... I didn't feel very well, we decided to leave early.

13 The money was hidden .... no-one could find it.

14 I'll come with you .... we don't stay late. I need to be up early tomorrow.

15 .... I like him, I sometimes find him very irritating.

55b Put an appropriate conjunction before the adverbial clauses. Write the answers in the spaces provided below the text.

The car: Is it worth it?

[1]..... the petrol-fuelled internal combustion engine was first developed by the German engineers Benz and Daimler in 1885, our lives have changed completely. [2]..... the damaging effects of the motor car are now well-recognized, the number of cars on the road continues to grow every year. In 1950, there were fewer than 50 million cars in use around the world, but [3]..... cars became more widely available and relatively cheaper, this number grew to 500 million by 1999.

We continue to drive cars [4]..... we know how dangerous they are in every respect. People seem to accept the higher number of deaths and injuries as a normal fact of life [5]..... smaller risks in other areas of life seem to generate more publicity and fear. We accept the awful risk [6]..... it is somehow justifiable. [7]..... any other activity carried with it such a risk, there would be a huge public reaction.

And what of the pollution? [8]..... research into car emissions started, it has become clearer and clearer how damaging the emissions are to health and the environment. Will we keep on driving our cars [9]..... much damage we do? It seems that people are [10]..... attached to their cars that they won't give them up for anything. To some people, their car is more important to them [11]..... anything else.

One of the obvious answers to the problem is better public transport. [12]..... we could travel [13]..... we liked on cheap, comfortable public transport, we would be less inclined to use the car. People will not stop using their cars [14]..... there is a good alternative. But we need to act now [15]..... it is too late. We must change our attitude and our priorities [16]..... future generations can live in a cleaner world.

1	*Since*..	9	....
2	....	10	....
3	....	11	....
4	....	12	....
5	....	13	....
6	....	14	....
7	....	15	....
8	....	16	....

56 Participial phrases

Check

56 In your notebook, write the following text changing clauses to participial phrases where possible.

Vincent Van Gogh, who was born in Holland in 1853, is one of the world's most famous painters. Although his talent was unrecognized throughout his life, it was much appreciated after his death.

After he had failed in every career he had attempted, Van Gogh first turned to art to express his strong religious feelings. After he had decided to become a painter, in about 1880, he started to paint studies of peasants and miners. During the next few years, which are known as his 'Dutch period', he produced paintings with rather dark greenish-brown colours.

In 1886, when he went to Paris to visit his brother Theo, he was immediately attracted to the Impressionist work he saw there. He decided to stay in Paris and continued his painting there. He was encouraged by Pissaro to use more colour in his pictures and his subsequent paintings were bright and immensely colourful.

After Van Gogh had moved to Arles in the south of France, in 1888, he worked frantically. This frenzied activity, which was interrupted by bouts of deep depression and despair, produced the majority of his most famous paintings. One of these, which is called *Self Portrait with Bandaged Ear*, shows Van Gogh: he was wearing a bandage after he had cut off his own ear. A year later, in 1890, he committed suicide.

A lot is known about Van Gogh's life and his feelings because of the hundreds of letters which were written by him to his brother Theo and others. Because his brother believed in Van Gogh's genius, he always encouraged him in his work. He was the person closest to Van Gogh.

Example:
Born in Holland in 1853, Vincent Van Gogh is one of the world's most famous painters.

57 Defining relative clauses

Look at this sentence:
The family who live next door moved here from Ireland.
There is a main clause: ***The family** ... **moved here from Ireland*** and there is a relative clause: ***who live next door***.

The main clause does not make proper sense without the relative clause. The relative clause tells us which family we are talking about. It is a defining relative clause.

The relative clause may come in the middle or at the end of a sentence. It follows the word that it defines.

- Subject relative pronouns:
  *Are you the person **who** telephoned here an hour ago?*
  The relative pronoun ***who*** functions as the subject of the verb *telephoned.*
  *Can you pick up the knife **that/which** has just fallen off the table?*
  The relative pronoun ***that/which*** functions as the subject of the verb *has fallen off*. ***That*** is used more often than ***which***. ***Which*** is more formal or scientific.

- Object relative pronouns:
  *That's the woman **who/that** I met at Tony's house.*
  Who or ***that*** functions as the object of the verb *met*.

  *Is this the book **that/which** you were reading last night?*
  That or ***which*** functions as the object of the verb *were reading*.

  In defining relative clauses, the object relative pronoun (***who/that/which***) is often omitted:
  That's the woman I met at Tony's house.
  Is this the book you were reading last night?

- Relative pronouns: object of a preposition:
  *This is the beach (**that/which**) I was telling you <u>about</u>.*
  That or ***which*** functions as the object of the preposition *about*. It can be omitted.

- Possessive relative pronoun:
  *They are the workers **whose** jobs are being cut.*
  Whose is a possessive relative pronoun. It refers to the workers. It is the workers' jobs that are being cut. ***Whose jobs*** functions as the subject of the verb *are being cut*.

  *I couldn't find the man **whose** case I'd taken by mistake.*
  Whose refers to the man. It was his case I'd taken. ***Whose case*** functions as the object of the verb *had taken*.

- Summary: relative pronouns in defining relative clauses:

	Subject	*Object*	*Possessive*
For people	<u>who</u>/that	<u>no pronoun</u>/who/that	whose
For things	<u>that</u>/which	<u>no pronoun</u>/that/which	—

Note: Where there is a choice of pronoun, the underlined one is the most commonly used.

Practice

57a Underline the ten defining relative clauses in the dialogue. Then circle the relative pronoun in each one and indicate whether it is a subject (S) or object (O) pronoun.

Holt and Watkins, private detectives, are discussing a murder.

W: So who was the one *who killed Mr Makepeace? (S)*

H: Can't you guess?

W: Well, I think it was probably the woman who was staying in the room next door to him.

H: No, Watkins, of course it wasn't. She only wanted the money he owed her. She won't get that now that he's dead.

W: Oh yes, I hadn't thought about that. So was it Mr Grant, the man who always shared their table in the evenings?

H: No, Watkins. It's true that he loved Mrs Makepeace but he knew that she didn't love him. And he probably believed that she could never fall in love with a man who had murdered her husband.

W: I suppose that's true. So who was it then? The son? Do you think that he wanted to have the money that would be due to him from his father's life insurance policy.

H: Well no, because he knew that the insurance policy would be invalid if his father died suspiciously. And apart from that, I think that in a way he loved his father. The one he hates is Mr Bottomley, the man his mother is in love with.

W: So who did kill Mr Makepeace?

H: Well, I feel quite sure now that it was Mrs Makepeace.

W: Mrs Makepeace!

H: Yes. She had never loved the man she had married. What she loved was all the money he had. Then Mr Bottomley came along. He had money too and she loved him. But she had to get Mr Makepeace out of the way.

57b Join the two sentences together, making the second sentence a defining relative clause. Use the relative pronoun that is most commonly used or no pronoun at all where this is possible.

1 She's the one. I told you about her.

She's the one I told you about.

2 I don't like the people. They are staying with the Browns.

....

....

3 I like books. They make you think about things.

....

....

4 I'm looking for the person. I've just hit their car.

....

....

5 Most of the books are still popular today. I read them as a child.

....

....

6 You can buy the pasta from that Italian shop. It has just opened in the high street.

....

....

7 The woman is coming back to work soon. I'm doing her job.

....

....

8 Is she the new television presenter? Everyone's talking about her.

....

....

9 People often have very little money to spend on leisure. They have a lot of leisure time.

....

....

10 Is Technico the company? Sarah works for them.

....

....

11 This is the job. I've always wanted it.

....

....

12 The swimming pool is only open to the public in the mornings. I use it.

....

....

13 We've just bought a computer package. It teaches you how to play the piano.

....

....

14 My favourite holiday was that one. We spent it in a cottage in the mountains.

....

....

15 We haven't seen the friends for ten years. They are coming to visit us this weekend.

....

....

58 Non-defining relative clauses

Look at the difference between these two sentences:

1 *The boy* <u>*who lives next door*</u> *is having a party tonight.*
The underlined clause is a defining relative clause. It tells us which boy is being talked about.
There are no commas before and after a defining relative clause.

2 *Darren,* <u>*who lives next door,*</u> *is having a party tonight.*
The underlined clause is a non-defining relative clause. It does not tell us which boy we are talking about; we already know that from the name. It gives us extra information about Darren.
A non-defining relative clause in the middle of a sentence has a comma before and after it. A non-defining relative clause at the end of a sentence has a comma before it and a full stop at the end.

- Subject relative pronouns:

  This is my friend Jane, ***who*** *has just returned from Italy.*
  The relative pronoun ***who*** refers to *Jane* and it functions as the subject of the verb *has … returned* in the relative clause.

  Mike's car, ***which*** *is only six months old, broke down last night.*
  The relative pronoun ***which*** refers to *Mike's car* and it functions as the subject of the verb *is* in the relative clause.

- Object relative pronouns:
  The woman next door, ***who/whom*** *I met for the first time last week, is moving next month.*
  Who or ***whom*** refer to *the woman next door* and function as the object of the verb *met* in the relative clause.
  Whom is more formal and is generally used in formal written English.
  Who is more common in spoken English.

Unlike the object relative pronoun in defining relative clauses, the object relative pronoun in non-defining relative clauses cannot be omitted.
*That book about the First World War, **which** I finished last week, was really interesting.*
Which refers to *that book about the First World War* and functions as the object of the verb *finished* in the relative clause. We cannot omit it.

- Relative pronouns: object of a preposition:
  a) *Marjorie Campbell, **who/whom** we have all depended <u>on</u> so much, has just announced her retirement.*
  b) *Marjorie Campbell, <u>on</u> **whom** we have all depended so much, has just announced her retirement.*

  Who or ***whom*** in sentence a) and ***whom*** in sentence b) refer to *Marjorie Campbell* and function as the object of the preposition *on*.

  a) *The new pedestrian crossings, **which** there has been much discussion <u>about</u>, are going to be in use from the beginning of next month.*
  b) *The new pedestrian crossings, <u>about</u> **which** there has been much discussion, are going to be in use from the beginning of next month.*

  Which refers to the new pedestrian crossings and functions as the object of the preposition *about*.

Notes:

- Position of preposition: In the a) sentences, the preposition comes at the end of the relative clause. This is less formal and is becoming more common.
  In the b) sentences, the preposition comes before the relative pronoun. This word order is used in more formal written English.
- ***Who*** or ***whom***? When the preposition comes before the relative pronoun, it is only possible to use ***whom*** for people. When the preposition comes at the end of the relative clause, it is possible to use ***who*** or ***whom***.

- Possessive relative pronoun:
  *Amanda Lovelace, **whose** husband died last year, has now lost her job.*
  Whose refers to *Amanda Lovelace*. It is her husband who died.
  Whose husband functions as the subject of the verb *died*.

  *This is our son John, **whose** friends you will be meeting at the party later on.*
  Whose refers to *our son John*. It is his friends you will be meeting.
  Whose friends functions as the object of the verb *will be meeting*.

  a) *We are hoping for a visit from Henry Webster, whose support we have so much depended <u>on</u>.*
  b) *We are hoping for a visit from Henry Webster, <u>on</u> **whose** support we have so much depended.*

  Whose support functions as the object of the preposition *on*. The preposition can go at the end of the relative clause, or it can go before the relative pronoun, which is quite formal. It is more common to put it at the end of the relative clause.

- Summary:

	For people	*For things*	*For possession*
Subject	who	which	whose
Object	who/whom	which	whose

Note: Spoken versus written English:
Non-defining relative clauses which are in the middle of a sentence are quite formal and are more commonly used in written English than in spoken English. In spoken English, we usually prefer to use shorter sentences or to link clauses together with simple conjugations. For example, in written English, we may write:
Ann Roberts, whose first job was in this department, has just been appointed Director.
but in spoken English, we are more likely to say something like:
Ann Roberts has just been appointed Director. Do you remember? Her first job was here in this department.

Practice

58a In your notebook, rewrite the sentences making the second sentence into a non-defining relative clause and putting it into the correct place.

1 When I was in town, I met your sister. She was shopping for some clothes.
When I was in town, I met your sister, who was shopping for some clothes.
2 Their house needs a lot of work doing to it. It is near the beach.
3 Sandra's just got a new job with Capital Insurers. It's a much better company than the last one she worked for.
4 The new manager seems to be a very capable woman. I met her last week.

5 This case is full of books. I carried it all the way from the station.
6 The Games International Company has just gone bankrupt. We have done business with them for many years.
7 The hospital has handed out redundancy notices to all its staff. It is due to close down next year.
8 The prisoners are requesting more time out of their cells. Their families are campaigning on their behalf.
9 The new government is now facing major problems. It came to power with a lot of public support.
10 Her latest novel is really good. I read it on holiday.
11 The Home Affairs Minister is suspected of being involved in a financial scandal. The opposition have accused the minister of lying.
12 The Education Department is changing its policy on single sex schools. Mrs Parkinson is in charge of the department.
13 The Lilley and Swan department store has made reductions on most of its goods. The store has a sale on at the moment.

14 The principal actor could hardly speak last night due to a sore throat. He normally has a wonderful voice.
15 The sales manager is planning a new advertising campaign. I support her ideas.

58b Use the sentences in the box to make non-defining relative clauses. Insert an appropriate clause into each of the sentences.

Her books are read all over the world. It was very crowded. We love to walk round them. ~~It is very powerful~~. He is staying in a nursing home. I like her very much. He is staying in his holiday home in Scotland at the moment. Her parents believed it. She came over to apologize to us. I always attend her lectures.

1 This new drug could have bad side effects.
This new drug, which is very powerful, could have bad side effects.

2 Her father is said to be dying of cancer.

....

....

3 The Prime Minister said that he was very saddened by the news of the air crash.

....

....

4 The story she gave was that she had not realized how late it was.

....

....

5 Agatha Christie was a very prolific writer.

....

....

6 The sub-tropical gardens are open all year round.

....

....

7 The manager of the restaurant said that she was very sorry about the undercooked fish.

....

....

8 Our Professor of Psychology has written some very interesting books.

....

....

9 We packed a picnic and walked down to the beach.

....

....

10 Next Saturday, I'm going to visit my Aunty Sheila.

....

....

59 Defining and non-defining relative clauses

Check

59 Underline all the relative clauses in the following article.

POETRY AND THE WAR

One of the most extraordinary things about the First World War was the enthusiasm with which the majority of soldiers went off to fight for their country. Those young, patriotic men, who rushed to the enlistment centres, had no idea what lay ahead of them. They did not know that they would live for months in holes they had dug in the mud. They did not know what it would be like to watch a friend who had been horribly injured die a painful death. And so they were excited, even thrilled, about the prospect of going to war.

This was the first war in which the image-makers made an impact. There were posters which asked women to encourage their men to go to war: 'If he does not think that you and your country are worth fighting for – do you think he is WORTHY of you?'

The mood which seized the country was one of patriotic and heroic struggle. At the same time, it was generally believed that it would all be over in a few months.

The war fever which gripped the nation stirred up the emotions of everyone and there was a huge growth in the writing of poetry. At first the poems were proud and optimistic: 'Now in thy splendour go before us Spirit of England', but as the war dragged on, the writers of poetry became angry at the myths they had been told. They wanted people to know about the horrible reality of war, which brutalized the people who took part.

One writer who put these feelings into words very effectively was Wilfrid Owen, who, in the poem Anthem for Doomed Youth, wrote 'What passing bells for these who die as cattle?' The poetry of Wilfrid Owen, Siegfried Sassoon, Robert Graves and others, which described the horrific reality of war, also questioned its morality. Many of the poets were wealthy, privileged men who had not at first been anti-war, but whose attitudes were changed by what they saw.

60 Relative clauses of time, place and reason

In relative clauses of time, place and reason, it is possible to use ***when***, ***where*** and ***why*** in place of relative pronouns.

- Time:
  1990 was (the year) ***when we moved here****.*
- Place:
  That's (the place) ***where we stayed for our honeymoon****.*

- Reason:
  Its central location is (the reason) ***why we chose this flat****.*

Note: Relative clauses with ***when***, ***where*** and ***why*** are usually defining but can be non-defining. Relative clauses starting with ***where*** are more often non-defining than relative clauses starting with ***when*** or ***why***:
The village of Baydon, ***where I lived as a child****, has now become part of the town.*

Practice

60 In your notebook, rewrite each pair of sentences as one sentence, using a relative clause with ***when***, ***where*** or ***why***.

1 The early morning is the time. I work best then.
The early morning is (the time) when I work best.
2 His mid-teens were the time. He first became interested in politics then.
3 His dishonesty is the reason. That's why I left him.
4 Edinburgh is the city. I'd most like to live there.
5 The outdoor swimming pool has now been closed down. We often went there as children.
6 This is a picture of the place. We're going there for our holidays.
7 His refusal to tell her the truth is the reason. That's why she is so angry with him.
8 This is the place. I fell off my bike here.
9 The people I work with are the reason. That's why I stay in the job.
10 That terrible night in December changed my life forever. I found out then what had been going on.

61 Relative clauses after *all*, etc.

- *All, anyone/anything, everyone/everything, the only thing, the best* (and other superlatives) + a defining relative clause:

*All **that happened** was that they had a little argument.*	Subject relative clause
*All **(that) I need to do now** is to buy my ticket.*	Object relative clause
*Everyone **who came to the party** really enjoyed it.*	Subject relative clause
*Everyone **(who/that) I met** said they were enjoying themselves.*	Object relative clause

Note: After ***everyone/anyone*** we can use ***who*** or ***that*** in both subject and object relative clauses.

- *A few, several, some, many, much, most, all, none, either/neither, half, a number, the biggest* (and other superlatives) + ***of whom/which*** in a non-defining relative clause:
  *My two cousins, **neither of whom I have seen for ten years**, are coming to visit next week.*
  *Her old letters, **some of which have now been lost**, make very interesting reading.*

Practice

61 In your notebook, put the following into one sentence using a relative clause.

1 You shouldn't listen to anything. He says it.
You shouldn't listen to anything (that) he says.
2 It was nice to see all his family. I have met most of them before.
It was nice to see all his family, most of whom I have met before.
3 The worst thing is that we'll miss the train. This can happen.
4 I've read both the reports. I agree with neither of them.
5 The only thing is to get some cash out of the bank. I need to do it.
6 The cleaners have decided to take industrial action. Several of them have complained to me about their low pay.
7 Everything has been a failure. I've done it.
8 I've lost any optimism for the future. I once had optimism.
9 Members of the committee have decided to call for an investigation. Many of them are themselves suspected of corruption.
10 The only thing is to give her the chance to talk about it. I can do that.
11 Everyone said that Peter started it. They saw the argument.
12 Those chocolates were not meant to be for me. I've already eaten half of them.
13 The management team are all saying the same thing. I trust none of them.
14 The cheapest was about £5, I saw it.
15 Her brothers have set up in business together. The youngest one is a friend of mine.

62 Co-ordinating relative clauses

- In a co-ordinating relative clause, ***which*** refers back to a whole sentence:
  *He has decided to see the doctor about it, **which is a good idea**.*
  Which refers back to him seeing the doctor about it.
- Co-ordinating relative clauses are always non-defining.

Practice

62 In your notebook, write sentences with a co-ordinating relative clause. Use the sentences in the box to make the relative clauses and combine them with the statements below.

It will be an interesting experience for him. That's just what she needs after all her problems. He should have done that a long time ago. It is very worrying. It will be a great help to him. It was a complete surprise. It is a terrible accusation to make. That will give him more time to spend with his girlfriend. That's why I don't go out very much. ~~It's a great shame~~.

1. She's going to have to sell the business.
   She's going to have to sell the business, which is a great shame.
2. The weather's very cold at this time of year.
3. He's decided to go and teach abroad.
4. They say he's been stealing money from the company.
5. She's going to have a month off work.
6. He's going to give up his evening job.
7. The editor has finally agreed to print an apology.
8. She suddenly appeared on the doorstep last night.
9. A few people have been attacked in this area recently.
10. He's going to have an electric wheelchair soon.

63 Tag questions

FORM

Tag questions are formed with the auxiliary of the verb in the main clause. For example, where the main verb is in the present simple, the tag is formed with ***does/do*** and where the verb is past simple, the tag is formed with ***did***. Where the main verb is positive, the tag is usually negative and where the main verb is negative, the tag is usually positive.
The majority of tag questions use a *falling* intonation.

*It's very cold, **isn't it**?*

*She comes from France, **doesn't she**?*

*I gave you the message, **didn't I**?*

Types of tag questions

Tag questions with a falling intonation

positive statement – negative tag
negative statement – positive tag

This is the most common type of tag question. The tag question is not really a question. We use it to make a comment where it is assumed that the listener agrees with the statement.

A statement on its own expresses an opinion to the listener or gives the listener some information. A statement with a tag question usually sounds more friendly because the tag assumes that the listener already knows this information or holds this opinion. When we use a tag question, we are therefore including the listener more in what we are saying.

The listener is expected to reply in agreement. S/he may reply in the following ways:
Statement with tag question: *It's a lovely day, **isn't it**?*

Short answer:	*Yes, it is.*
Short answer with additional comment:	*Yes, it is. It's much nicer than yesterday.*
Short answer with another tag question:	*Yes, it is, **isn't it**?*

USE

- To make a single conversational statement:

  *(It's a) Lovely day, **isn't it**?*

  *It's not very nice today, **is it**?*

  *The train's late today, **isn't it**?*

- To open a conversation and introduce a topic:

  It was terrible news about that murder, ***wasn't it****?*

  It looks like this meeting's going to be interesting, ***doesn't it****?*

  This year's pay review hasn't been announced yet, ***has it****?*

- To pass a comment during a conversation:

  Yes, it's disgusting, ***isn't it****?*

  But he made some very good points, ***didn't he****?*

Tag questions with a rising intonation

positive statement – negative tag
negative statement – positive tag

Tag questions with a rising intonation are much less common than tag questions with a falling intonation. A tag with a rising intonation is more questioning than a tag with a falling intonation. It expresses stronger feelings than a falling tag and can be used to convey a range of emotions.

USE

- To express surprise or disapproval:

  You didn't tell him, ***did you****?*

- To express surprise and ask for confirmation of what the speaker thought to be true:

  A: *I think he's taking his test next week.*

  B: *But he passed his test a long time ago,* ***didn't he****?*

- To check and ask for confirmation:

  That's your car, ***isn't it****?*

- To make a tentative polite request:

  You couldn't open the door for me, ***could you****?*

- To express suspicion:

  It wasn't you who told him, ***was it****?*

Tag questions with a rising intonation

positive statements - positive tag

These tags are not so common as positive-negative or negative-positive tags. The tag can convey a range of emotions.

USE

- To express friendly interest and to encourage the other speaker to give more information:

  So, you've been given a promotion, ***have you****?*

- To make a suggestion, where agreement is expected:

  We'll go for a swim this afternoon, ***shall we****?*

- To express disagreement and a warning:

  So you think you're tougher than me, ***do you****?*

- To express disapproval and an accusation:

  You went there without telling me, ***did you****?*

Echo tags

Positive statement – positive echo tag
Negative statement – negative echo tag

Intonation: falling or rising
Rising intonation expresses more surprise.

An echo tag is a tag used in response to a statement.
Echo tags are very common in spoken English.
We use echo tags to show that we are listening to what the speaker is saying and showing interest:
A: *I met David the other night.*
B: ***Did you?***

A: *I'm not going to apply for that job now.*
B: ***Aren't you?***

Notes

- Tag questions always use a pronoun and not a full name:
  John's coming, ***isn't he****?*
  NOT ~~*John's coming,* ***isn't John****?*~~
  and NOT ~~*He's coming,* ***isn't John****?*~~
- When the main sentence has a modal, use the modal in the tag:
  You can help me, ***can't you****?*
  James would have helped us, ***wouldn't he****?*
- When the subject of the sentence is ***there***, use ***there*** in the tag:
  There aren't many people here, ***are there****?*
- When the subject of the sentence is ***This/That***, use ***it*** in the tag:
  That's nice, ***isn't it****?*

- When the subject of the sentence is ***These/Those***, use ***they*** in the tag:
  Those are beautiful, ***aren't they****?*
- When the subject of the sentence is a word like ***no-one***, ***someone***, ***everyone***, the tag uses the pronoun ***they***:
  Everyone's coming tonight, ***aren't they****?*
- Sentences with negative subjects like ***nothing***, ***no-one***, ***neither***, ***anyone*** behave like negative sentences and have a positive tag:
  Nobody saw you, ***did they****?*
  I don't think anyone's coming, ***are they****?*
- Imperative sentences use ***will*** in the tag:
  Don't do that again, ***will you****?*
- Sentences with ***Let's*** ... use ***shall*** in the tag:
  Let's go there tomorrow, ***shall we****?*
- Negative questions can perform a similar function to question tags with a falling intonation.
  It's cold today, ***isn't it****?*
  Isn't it cold today?

Practice

63a Complete the gaps with a tag question or echo tag.

A: It's been a wonderful day, 1 hasn't it ?

B: Yes, fantastic. And we've had no problems with anything, 2.................................... ? Everything's been perfect.

A: That's right. It'll certainly be a lovely day to remember, 3.................................... ?

****

A: I had a letter from Louis yesterday.

B: Oh, 4.................................... ?

A: Yes, he says he's coming to stay this weekend.

B: Really? That'll be nice, 5.................................... ?

****

A: I don't know what to do today. Just look at the rain outside.

B: Well, I don't want to stay in all day. Let's go and see a film, 6.................................... ?

A: Why not? Good idea. There's nothing much on at the local cinema though, 7.................................... ?

B: All right. We'll take the train into town then, 8.................................... ?

****

A: Eve and Tony are coming round for dinner tonight.

B: 9.................................... ? Oh, that'll be nice.

A: Yes. I thought you might like to come too.

B: Well yes, but you haven't seen them for a long time. I expect you'd like to talk to them on your own, [10]...................................... ?

****

A: How did you get in here?

B: I came in through the back door.

A: Nobody saw you coming in, [11]...................................... ?

B: No, I don't think so.

A: You shouldn't come and see me like this. It's dangerous. Please don't come here again, [12]...................................... ?

****

A: That's a beautiful table, [13]...................................... ?

B: Yes, it is, [14]...................................... ?

A: It would be lovely in our kitchen, [15]...................................... ? Why don't we get it?

B: Don't be ridiculous. Look at the price. We can't afford it, [16]...................................... ?

****

A: You couldn't hold this door open for me, [17]...................................... ? I can't get the pram through it.

B: Of course. It's terrible how they design these doors, [18]...................................... ? It makes it so difficult for people in wheelchairs or with young children.

A: Yes, it does, [19]...................................... ?

****

A: I've just been talking to Roger.

B: [20]..................................... , Dad?

A: Yes, and I didn't like what he told me. So you went to that nightclub on Friday, [21]..................................... ? The one I told you not to go to.

B: I'm sorry Dad. I thought you wouldn't really mind.

A: Oh you did, [22]..................................... ? Well, I do mind.

63b In your notebook, rewrite the conversation adding tag questions where appropriate.

Tracey and Dominic used to be girlfriend and boyfriend. They meet again at a party.

D: Hello. Nice to see you here. It's a great party.
T: Yes, it's really good. There are so many people here that I haven't seen for ages.
D: Yes, there are a lot of our old school crowd here. Have you spoken to many of them?
T: Yes, quite a few. I bumped into Adrian a few minutes ago and we had a brief chat. Well, no, he chatted and I listened.
D: Yes, he's still the same. He just loves talking about himself and he doesn't seem to be interested in what anyone else has to say.
T: That's right. Oh look, that's Melanie over there.
D: Yes, you're right, it is. Who's that she's with?
T: It's Matthew.
D: But he's going out with her sister Emma.
T: Well, yes, I thought so. But look, he's holding Melanie's hand.
D: Oh yes. Well, I suppose our information must be out-of-date then. Anyway, what about you? I've missed you, you know.
T: Yes, I've missed you too.
D: But I expect you've got a new boyfriend now.
T: Not now. I did for a little while after you went away but not now.
D: It was hard saying goodbye. I was going to write to you but I thought it wouldn't help.
T: No, maybe not. Well, anyway, we're here together now. Why don't we just enjoy ourselves.
D: Good idea. Let's dance.
T: Yes, I'd like to. But not now. The music's terrible.
D: Well, it's no good for dancing, that's for sure. We'll go and ask them if we can change it.
T: OK. Well, you go. And put on one of our favourites.
D: Yes, I will. And you will be waiting for me when I get back?
T: Yes, of course I will.

Example: *D: Hello. Nice to see you here. It's a great party, isn't it?*

64 Common prepositions of time

at	a time: ***at*** *9 o'clock* an age: ***at*** *fifteen/the age of fifteen*
on	a day or a date: ***on*** *Monday,* ***on*** *25th September* ***on*** *Saturday afternoon,* ***on*** *the morning of 4th June* + noun/gerund: ***On*** *departure/departing, she …* = *When she departed, she …*
in	a period of time: – some time during that period: ***in*** *the morning,* ***in*** *February,* ***in*** *1994* – at the end of a stated period: *I'll be ready* ***in*** *five minutes.* (five minutes from now) – the length of time that something takes: *I read the book* ***in*** *two and a half hours.*
by	a time, date, period, not later than that time: *You must be here* ***by*** *7 o'clock.*
before	a time, date, period, event: *I never go to bed* ***before*** *midnight.*
after	a time, date, period, event: *I'll phone you* ***after*** *lunch.*
since	a point in time, from that time until now or until a point in the past: *We've been here* ***since*** *Tuesday.* *It was the end of the summer. They had been there* ***since*** *June.*
for	a period of time: *They've been together* ***for*** *three years.*
during	a named period or an event: *We always work hard* ***during*** *the summer.* *Fighting broke out between rival fans* ***during*** *the match.*
until/till	a point in time, the point in time at which the action finished: *We slept* ***until/till*** *8.00.* *We didn't wake up* ***until/till*** *8.00.*
from a time **to/until/till** a time:	*We slept* ***from*** *11.30* ***to/until/till*** *8.00.*

Notes

- We use ***at*** with festivals and religious celebrations: ***at*** *Easter*
- We say ***at night***. But we can also say ***in the night*** meaning *during*.
- We often use ***last/this/next*** with time words:
  We didn't go on holiday ***last*** *summer.*
  I'm going home ***this*** *weekend.*
  I'll see you ***next*** *Monday.*
- ***During*** versus ***for***:
  We rented a cottage ***for*** *the summer.*
  (Tells us how long)

*He became ill **during** the summer.*
(Tells us when – at some point in the summer period)

*We spend all our time outside **during** the summer.*
(Tells us when – refers to the whole summer period)

- ***During*** versus ***in***:
  They can both be used to refer to something that happens throughout a time period, from its beginning to its end, and so it is often possible to use either ***during*** or ***in***.
  *It's very cold here **during/in** the winter.*

  BUT
  - We use ***in*** and not ***during*** when we want the time reference to sound more specific. So, for example, if we are contrasting one period of time with another, we use ***in***:
    *I last saw you **in** May, not July.*
  - We use ***during*** when we want to stress the idea of duration.
    *She felt miserable **during** the whole of that summer.*
  - When the time reference is an activity rather than a time period, we use ***during***:
    *She didn't speak once **during** the meal.*

Practice

64 Complete the gaps with a suitable preposition of time.

Paula and Jemma are friends.

P: Jemma, how would you like to come round for a meal [1]..on.. Saturday?

J: Yes, that sounds a good idea. [2].................. the evening, do you mean?

P: Yes. [3].................. about 8 o'clock if that's O.K.

J: Sure, that would be fine. The only thing is, I'll have to leave [4].................. about midnight because I've got to get up early [5]......... Sunday morning.

P: That's all right. I don't like staying up much [6].................. midnight anyway.

J: No, neither do I. I stayed up [7].................. three o'clock last Saturday and I felt terrible [8].................. Sunday morning.

P: So what were you doing [9].................. three o'clock?

J: Oh, Kirsty came down [10].................. the weekend. We actually got home [11].................. about half past twelve [12].................. Saturday night but then we stayed up talking [13].................. another two and a half hours.

P: Oh, how is Kirsty? I haven't seen her [14].................. your party last year.

J: Oh, she's a bit fed up. She's just split up with Matthew [15].................. four years together.

P: Oh, poor Kirsty.

J: Yes, and they split up just [16].................. her exams started too. In fact, I think she had her first exam the next day. Isn't that awful? Anyway, I'll tell you about it [17].................. Saturday.

P: O.K. I'll see you then.

65 Common prepositions of position and movement

- *(away)* ***from/at/to*** a place.
  Use when the reason for being there is more important than the exact position. It may be inside or outside:
  I'll meet you ***at*** *the station.*
  We walked ***from*** *the station* ***to*** *the cinema.*
- ***out of/in/in(to)*** a place.
  Use when the place is something with walls or boundaries:
  I'll wait for you ***in*** *the car.*
  Could you get ***in(to)*** *the car?*
  Can I get ***out of*** *the car here, please?*
- ***off/on/on(to)*** a surface or line:
  We need some pictures ***on*** *the wall.*
  Shall we take that picture ***off*** *the wall?*
  Do you think we should put this ***on*** *the wall?*

Note: We usually use ***on*** rather than ***onto***. We use ***onto*** when we want to emphasize the movement from one place onto another:
I drove ***onto*** *the motorway.* (I drove off another road and onto the motorway.)
I drove ***on*** *the motorway.* (That's where I drove./That's how I got there.)

Notes:
- arrive ***at/in*** a place
  get ***to/into*** a place
  get ***in*** (without place)
  in as an adverb: *When does the train get* ***in****?*
- ***on*** a train, bus, plane
  in a car

Practice

65 Complete the gaps with a preposition (or adverb) of position or movement. Two friends, Polly and Maria, are talking.

P: I didn't see you [1].*at*. the club last night. Where were you? Did you stay [2]............. home?

M: Yes, I thought it was time to stay [3]............. for a change and, besides, I didn't feel very well. I just lay [4]............. the bath reading for ages. I decided I wasn't going to get [5]............. the bath until I'd finished the book. But then Rosie turned up [6]............. the doorstep so I had to get [7]............. to see her.

P: So are you feeling well enough to come out later on?

M: I think so.

P: Well, I'm going round [8]............. Helen's at 5.00 and we're going to take the train [9]............. Highbury [10]............. Richmond. So we should get [11]............. Richmond by 6.00. Then we can walk [12]............. the station [13]............. that nice café [14]............. the riverbank. And if we see Charles there, he might invite us [15]............. his boat.

M: Oh, that would be nice.

P: Did he tell you about Kate pushing him [16]............. last week?

M: No. So, he fell [17]............. the boat, did he?

P: Yes, and straight [18]............. the river. He was soaked, and pretty cold too.

66 Prepositions of time, position and movement

Check

66 Complete the gaps with a suitable preposition or adverb of time or place.

It was 8 o'clock [1].*on*. a cold morning [2].................. January. She was still asleep. She usually stayed [3].................. bed [4].................. about 9 o'clock [5].................. the winter. Suddenly she was woken up by a knocking at the door. She got [6].................. bed and went [7].................. the door. There was a man [8].................. the doorstep. She thought she recognized him. 'Hello Edna,' he said. 'It's Tom. Can I come [9].................. ?' And then she knew who it was but she didn't quite believe it. She hadn't seen him [10].................. thirty years, not [11].................. the summer of 1940 when she'd said goodbye to him the night

[12]................... his final departure. That was when he went off [13]................... war. It was two years [14]................... that when she received the letter [15]................... the War Office which said that Tom had been missing [16]................... some time and was now presumed dead. She kept on hoping that they were wrong right up [17]................... the end of the war. But then she gave up. [18]................... then, she'd continued to think of Tom every day. [19]................... his birthday, she always stayed [20]................... home all day because she couldn't bear to meet anybody. She'd met Tom [21]................... the age of sixteen and they'd had a wonderful time together [22]................... the start of the war. She was nineteen when war broke out and they'd been together [23]................... three years. They were going to get married [24]................... the war.

She looked at his face. It was still the same face but with quite a few lines [25]................... it and there was a bit less hair [26]................... his head. He put his hand [27]................... his pocket and took out a small photograph. It was one she'd sent him just [28]................... his disappearance. It was a picture of her [29]................... a teenager [30]................... the war. She held it [31]................... her hand and remembered back to those times. She felt rather hot and dizzy and thought that she might fall [32]................... the floor at any moment. She asked him to come [33]................... the living-room and they sat down together to tell their stories.

Test 1

Part A

Fill in the gaps with ***a*** or ***an***, ***the*** or no article.

Dear William,

Hello from [1]........................... Mexico City! I'm staying at [2]........................... beautiful hotel in [3]........................... centre of [4]........................... city. This [5]........................... morning I had [6]........................... breakfast in [7]........................... hotel garden. Tomorrow I'm going to rent [8]........................... car and drive to [9]........................... mountains. I hope [10]........................... weather will be fine.

See you soon,

Carol

SCORING

Score ☐

10 points. *Give yourself one point for each correct answer.*

Part B

Put the words in these sentences in the correct order.

1 She bought a silk / new / lovely / blouse.

....

2 The shop sells old / expensive / handmade objects.

....

3 seldom / gets to work / 9.00 / she / before.

....

4 I'll / see him / probably / when I come to work / in the morning / early.

....

5 He left the house / after his phone call / suddenly / quite.

....

SCORING

Score ☐

5 points. *Give yourself one point for each completely correct answer.*

Part C

Use the comparative or superlative form of the adjectives and adverbs in brackets.

A: Do you like your new job?

B: Oh, yes, it's much [1]............................ (interesting) than my old position. Of course, I have to work [2]............................ (hard), too.

A: Are the working conditions [3]............................ (good), too?

B: My office is [4]............................ (spacious), and it's [5]............................ (quiet). But the people in my old office were [6]............................ (friendly). My new boss seems [7]............................ (difficult) to please, too.

A: Well, you're [8]............................ (new) person, so I guess you'll have to prove yourself.

B: I'm certainly working much [9]............................ (hard) than anyone else in the office! It's a real challenge, but every day it gets [10]................. (easy).

SCORING Score ☐

10 points. *Give yourself one point for each correct answer.*

Part D

Put the verbs in brackets into the correct present or past form (present; past; present perfect; past perfect). You may use both simple and continuous aspects.

A: How long [1]........................... (you/work) there?

B: For three years. I [2]........................... (leave) last year.

A: [3]........................... (you/meet) Sarah?

B: Oh, yes, I [4]........................... (know) her for several months. She [5]........................... (be) in my dance class. We [6]........................... (go) to the same class every Tuesday since January.

A: [7]........................... (the phone/ring?)

B: Yes, but I [8]........................... (cook) dinner, so I [9]........................... (not/answer) it.

A: Why didn't you give him the news?

B: By the time I found out, he [10] .... (already/leave).

SCORING Score ☐

10 points. *Give yourself one point for each correct answer.*

Part E

Put the verbs in brackets into the correct future tense (*going to*; *will/shall*; present form).

A: Do you have any plans for tomorrow?

B: We [1]................................... (take) the children to the park.

A: I heard on the radio that it [2]................................... (rain).

B: Oh. If it rains, then I guess we [3]................................... (stay) home. If we [4]................................... (stay) home, I [5]................................... (call) you and invite you over to watch a video with us.

SCORING

Score ☐

5 points. *Give yourself one point for each correct answer.*

Part F

Combine each phrase in column A with a suitable phrase from column B. Not all phrases in column B will be used.

	A	B
1	He got the job despite	kind and thoughtful.
2	She was quite nervous, so	he had so much experience.
3	He seems well-educated; however,	I don't like her.
4	I hired him because	she didn't do very well.
5	She is not only beautiful and intelligent but	not having much experience.
		he's not very bright.
		not very interesting.

1 ....

2 ....

3 ....

4 ....

5 ....

SCORING

Score ☐

5 points. *Give yourself one point for each correct answer.*

Part G

Choose a preposition from the box to fill the gaps. Not all prepositions will be used.

about	after	at	beyond	during	in	onto	out	to	until

Today was definitely not my lucky day! First, when I got [1]................. the bus, I bumped my head. When I got [2]................. work, my boss yelled at me. [3]................. a phone call, I spilled coffee on some important papers; [4]................. that, I accidentally deleted some important files on my computer. My bad luck continued [5]................. I went home. I hope tomorrow is a better day.

SCORING
5 points. *Give yourself one point for each correct answer.*

Score ☐

TOTAL SCORE
Maximum 50 points. *Add up your score.*

Total Score ☐

Test 2

Part A

Underline the correct verb forms to complete the sentences.

1 By this summer, I **will have been working / will be working** here for 5 years.
2 I **will have to finish / will have had to finish** washing the car before I can go out.
3 You are **not to speak / not to be speaking** during the test.
4 **Will you wait / Will you be waiting** for me when I return?
5 They **don't intend to marry / don't intend to marrying** until after they graduate.
6 Don't bother cleaning up; I **will do / will have done** it later.
7 She wishes her husband **doesn't come / didn't come** home so late every night.
8 I wish he **writes / wrote** to me more often.
9 If only he **knew / had known** the truth before he spoke to her.
10 I wish you **would stop / stopped making** that awful noise while I'm studying.

SCORING Score ☐

10 points. *Give yourself one point for each correct answer.*

Part B

Put the verbs in brackets into the passive where possible.

A report [1].. (just come in) that the Southgate warehouse [2].. (break into) last Friday night. The gate [3].. (force) open and two of the back windows [4].. (shatter). Someone, probably a tall male, [5].. (leave) muddy footprints in the back hall. The owners [6].. (tell) reporters that nothing terribly valuable [7].. (take); however, there is a lot of damage [8].. (repair). Police [9].. (work) on the case now, and expect an arrest [10].. (make) within a week.

SCORING Score ☐

10 points. *Give yourself one point for each correct answer.*

Part C

Answer the following questions by using one of the phrasal verbs from the box. Use the appropriate verb tense, and use pronouns in your answer where possible. Not all the verbs in the box will be used.

call up cheer up come up with fix up give up run out of save up take after turn down

1 A: Did you accept that job offer?

B: No, I ....

2 A: Does the baby look like his father?

B: No, actually, I think he .... his mother.

3 A: Have you had any good ideas for the project yet?

B: Yes, I've just .... something wonderful.

4 A: I didn't know you smoked.

B: Well, I .... for a few years, but then I started again.

5 A: What's the matter? Have we .... petrol?

B: No, the engine's overheating.

SCORING Score ☐

5 points. *Give yourself one point for each correct answer.*

Part D

Use a gerund or infinitive form of the verbs in brackets to complete the letter.

Dear Ms Collins,

I am writing [1]............................ (express) my interest in the secretarial position at CRS advertised in the Times last week. I am proficient at [2]............................ (type), and know how [3]............................ (use) most word-processing packages. I enjoy [4]............................ (work) with people, know how [5]............................ (meet) a challenge, and don't mind [6]............................ (work) overtime. As you can see from the enclosed letters of reference, my previous employers considered me [7]............................ (be) a skilled secretary. I would be pleased [8]............................ (further) my career by [9]............................ (work) for a prestigious company like CRS. I look forward to [10]............................ (hear) from you.

Yours sincerely

Caroline Sinclair

SCORING Score ☐

10 points. *Give yourself one point for each correct answer.*

Part E

Rewrite the sentences below, using a present participle or a perfect participle. Where there are two sentences, join them to form one, using a participle.

1 He wore himself out. He hiked all day.

....

2 After we heard the news, we came over as quickly as possible.

....

3 She had worked hard all day. She wanted to go out for dinner.

....

4 Soon after he moved up north, he regretted his decision.

....

5 While I sympathize with your point of view, I cannot totally agree with you.

....

SCORING Score ☐

5 points. *Give yourself one point for each correct answer.*

Part F

Combine the two sentences into one, using a relative pronoun or a conjunction, and making any necessary changes.

1 That's the woman. Her dog bit me.

....

2 Can you tell me about the town? You were born there.

....

3 I found the book. It was taken from the library.

....

4 I can't remember the time. I first heard that song.

....

5 The woman married my best friend. The woman is my cousin.

....

SCORING Score ☐

5 points. *Give yourself one point for each correct answer.*

Part G

Add a tag question to each sentence.

1 You haven't seen my bag anywhere, ... ?

2 Laura couldn't have spoken to him this morning, ... ?

3 So, you went into my room when I was away, ... ?

4 The meeting went quite well, ... ?

5 Nobody is coming tonight, ... ?

SCORING Score ☐

5 points. *Give yourself one point for each correct answer.*

TOTAL SCORE Total Score ☐

Maximum 50 points. *Add up your score.*

Test 3

Part A

Put the verbs in brackets into the correct form.

1 If you .... (finish) your work, you could come with us. It doesn't look like it'll be done in time, though.

2 If it hadn't rained, the flowers .... (die).

3 I .... (not go) there if I were you.

4 If this water .... (not be) cleaned up, there's going to be an accident.

5 If you .... (go) to the lecture today, please take good notes.

6 You'll have to move if you .... (get) that promotion.

7 If the other driver had been looking, he .... (not hit) our car.

8 He .... (not come) to the party if Tessa is invited.

9 If the house .... (be) warmer, I wouldn't have to wear a jacket inside.

10 If you .... (be) more careful, you wouldn't have made so many mistakes.

SCORING — Score ☐

10 points. *Give yourself one point for each correct answer.*

Part B

Match the clauses by writing the letter of the second half in the space provided after the first half. No letter will be used twice.

1	You don't have to call me	a	if they hadn't offered me more money.
2	He wouldn't have been angry	b	as long as they offer me more money.
3	I won't work overtime	c	unless she apologizes to me.
4	I would take that job	d	if only you hadn't been so late.
5	I would have left my job last year	e	on condition that you are not late.
6	I wouldn't want to speak to her again	f	provided they offered me more money.
7	I will be happy to see her again	g	assuming that you're not late.
8	I won't go out with her again	h	even if they offer me more money.

9	We'll get there before the film begins	i	even if she apologized to me.
10	I will renew my contract for next year	j	as long as she apologizes to me.

SCORING — Score ☐

10 points. *Give yourself one point for each correct answer.*

Part C

Each sentence has one mistake. Rewrite the sentences, correcting the mistake.

1 I think this umbrella can be Emily's; she was carrying one like it yesterday.

....

....

2 After I've been studying French for another year, I can speak it more fluently.

....

....

3 We must to leave as soon as she gets here.

....

4 You ought write to your parents more often.

....

5 He isn't able to be very bright; he's failed the course three times.

....

6 I wish I can come to your party.

....

7 He must waits until the bank opens.

....

8 They'll have to taking a taxi to get there in time.

....

9 My parents say that I am able to stay out until midnight.

....

10 May I to use this phone to make a private call?

....

SCORING — Score ☐

10 points. *Give yourself one point for each correct answer.*

Part D

Choose a word from the box to complete each sentence. Each word is used once.

mustn't	need to	needn't	should	shouldn't

1 It's an airline regulation that you .... unfasten your seatbelt until the plane has landed.

2 If she wants to lose weight, she .... eat so many sweets.

3 You .... submit two photos with your application.

4 You .... have brought your umbrella: it's not going to rain.

5 He .... have thought more carefully before he spoke!

SCORING

Score ☐

5 points. *Give yourself one point for each correct answer.*

Part E

Underline the correct form of the infinitive or gerund in each sentence.

1 I hope **to be chosen / to be choosing** for the lead role in the play.
2 Please thank her for **having done / being done** such a fine job.
3 I deeply regret **having lied / to have lied** about the matter.
4 She would like **to have completed / to be completing** her courses before she gets married.
5 What do you expect **to have been doing / to be doing** in five years?

SCORING

Score ☐

5 points. *Give yourself one point for each correct answer.*

Part F

Rewrite the following sentences in reported speech. Use appropriate forms for written reporting.

1 'I am going to resign next month.'

The Councillor said that he .... next month.

2 'I didn't realize all the problems.'

She explained that she .... all the problems.

3 'There will be a few changes around the office.'

The boss announced that there .... a few changes around the office.

4 'Heavy rains have caused flooding in the north.'

The weather report mentioned that heavy rains .... flooding in the north.

5 'I have been playing the piano for 5 years.'

He told me that he .... the piano for 5 years.

6 'No, he's not employed.'

His wife explained that he .... employed.

7 'I completely forgot!'

He admitted that he ....

8 'We're having a dinner party this Wednesday.'

The Carters told us that they .... this Wednesday.

9 'By this summer, I will have been working there for three years.'

He told us that by this summer, he .... there for three years.

10 'I don't have enough time to finish.'

The student complained that she .... enough time to finish.

SCORING

Score ☐

10 points. *Give yourself one point for each correct answer.*

TOTAL SCORE

Total Score ☐

Maximum 50 points. *Add up your score.*

Key

1a tennis, squash, bowling, table tennis, snooker, equipment, tuition, coaching, competition, thirst, fruit juice, mineral water, footwear, lighting, sunlight, swimwear, exercise, food, food, fruit, bread, advice, information

1b 1 b 2 a 3 b 4 a 5 b 6 a 7 b 8 b 9 b 10 b 11 a 12 a 13 b 14 b 15 b

2a 1 the a 2 a the 3 The 4 – – 5 the the 6 the the 7 an an 8 – – 9 a 10 The – 11 – the 12 The the the 13 a – the 14 a the 15 an 16 the – 17 The the 18 The the 19 – 20 a a – the

2b 1 – 2 a 3 the 4 the 5 the 6 the 7 a 8 the 9 the 10 a 11 the 12 a 13 a 14 the 15 a 16 an 17 the 18 – 19 – 20 a 21 a 22 the 23 The 24 – 25 a 26 the 27 a 28 the 29 a 30 –

2c Timothy Harding has worked for this company for ten years. Throughout this time he has shown himself to be **a** hard-working and enthusiastic employee. He first joined **the** company as **a** junior sales representative but was soon promoted and is now at **the** head of **a** successful team of sales representatives. He manages **the** team with skill and energy and **the** significant increase in sales achieved by **the** team is **a** measure of his success. He has considerable initiative and this has been particularly evident in **the** area of training, where he has had notable success. **The** training programme he devised for his team has now been adopted throughout **the** company with very positive results.

On **a** personal level, I have found Timothy to be **a** very honest and considerate person and he is well-liked in **the** company. I have no hesitation in recommending him for **the** job for which he has applied, though I would of course be sorry to lose him.

3a 1 The holiday was absolutely wonderful. 2 They are staying in an enormous old grey building. 3 He looks rather tired and old now. 4 We met a charming young medical student. 5 He is an angry, aggressive young man. 6 He is a very heavy smoker. 7 She has made him very happy. 8 He gave her a beautiful, heavy gold necklace. 9 They are extremely close friends. 10 You seem rather unhappy at the moment. 11 He seems to be a very thoughtful young man. 12 The project is expensive, time-wasting and impractical. 13 My hair is beginning to turn grey. 14 Diana is a successful and well-respected young actress. 15 I am feeling fine now.

3b 1 relaxed 2 well-acted 3 embarrassing 4 boiling 5 well brought-up 6 broken 7 well-brushed 8 changing 9 clear-thinking 10 continuing 11 well-built 12 badly-planned 13 fast-declining 14 beautifully-tailored 15 dried 16 beautifully-kept 17 well-written 18 stolen 19 loving 20 parked

3c 1 enjoyable 2 forgetful 3 powerless 4 truthful 5 tireless 6 descriptive 7 reliable 8 submissive 9 careless 10 graceful 11 motionless 12 changeable 13 active 14 comfortable 15 dreadful

3d
dis- disagreeable distasteful dishonest
un- unattractive unjustified unfriendly uninteresting
il- illiterate illegal illegible illogical
im- impatient immature immoral impossible immortal imperfect impolite
in- inflexible inconvenient insignificant inexplicable indestructible insoluble inseparable
ir- irrelevant irregular irreplaceable irresponsible irrational irreversible

3e The first adjective in each pair is gradable: surprising, amazing; hungry, starving; nice, wonderful; dirty, filthy; upset, devastated; tasty, delicious; big, enormous; angry, furious; ugly, hideous; difficult, impossible; small, minute; frightened, terrified; good, perfect; tired, exhausted; thirsty, parched; important, vital; bad, terrible

4 1 lower 2 more disappointing 3 oldest 4 cheaper 5 most important 6 more efficient 7 more flexible 8 more worrying 9 more and more critical 10 biggest 11 highest 12 best 13 more spacious 14 best 15 better 16 less polluted 17 less stressful 18 quieter 19 more interesting 20 less varied 21 busier 22 less crowded 23 more excited 24 best 25 more settled 26 most beautiful

5a 1 I've been working hard in my office all morning. 2 He never speaks to me nicely in the mornings. 3 We were listening carefully all evening. 4 She's been sleeping soundly in that chair all afternoon. 5 He is usually at the college at this time of day. 6 The postman comes very early in the morning. 7 I thought you spoke very well in that meeting yesterday. 8 We generally go swimming at the local pool on Saturdays 9 I bought these jeans very cheaply in the sales last week. 10 He's never been to a dentist in his life.

5b 1 impatiently 2 already 3 for three hours 4 soon 5 for months 6 so much 7 hardly 8 deeply 9 absolutely 10 only 11 a few times 12 lovingly 13 in a friendly way 14 Suddenly 15 straightaway 16 just 17 anxiously

6a 1 more heavily 2 happier 3 harder 4 healthier 5 more suddenly 6 more expensive 7 more hungrily 8 hotter 9 more frequently 10 more seriously 11 more furious 12 more considerately 13 more assertively 14 colder 15 nicer 16 more tactfully 17 more cheaply 18 easier 19 more calmly

6b 1 as young as 2 more and more tired 3 as quickly as 4 less often 5 more enthusiastically 6 earlier 7 faster 8 more energetically 9 (more) optimistically 10 better

7a 1 's worrying 2 don't see 3 's been going on 4 went out 5 think 6 assumed 7 was interested 8 Have you told 9 doesn't seem 10 was working 11 came up 12 put 13 don't like 14 suppose 15 doesn't believe 16 's getting 17 'm getting 18 'm thinking 19 do you really want 20 don't want 21 's attending 22 expect 23 's talking 24 trying 25 dislike

7b 1 do you weigh 2 're having 3 's looking 4 admire 5 is appearing 6 are 7 represents 8 're thinking 9 Do you see 10 looks 11 'm seeing 12 don't have 13 do you think 14 's expecting 15 'm just admiring 6 're weighing 17 appears 18 's being 19 expect 20 is representing

8 1 has suffered 2 have worked 3 will have heard 4 had been 5 had had 6 will have been married 7 had already died 8 had certainly been 9 has happened 10 will have been 11 has fallen off 12 had all lost 13 will have finished 14 had decided 15 Have you found

9a
1 works … organises … is working … is going
2 are staying … belongs … is cycling … use … enjoy
3 is doing … are taking … need … are learning … are … are getting … provides … organises
4 is still increasing … are already starving … are suffering … is growing … need … die

9b 1 don't think 2 are you getting on 3 's going 4 Are you still going out 5 'm going out 6 's talking 7 see 8 Is he wearing 9 looks 10 comes 11 's life treating 12 'm still working 13 keep 14 feel 15 get in 16 don't have 17 suppose 18 hope 19 's coming over 20 Do you want

10a 1 was 2 was 3 were screaming 4 shouting 5 wanted 6 was pouring 7 was dripping 8 was thumping 9 loved 10 felt 11 decided 12 started 13 went 14 were all dancing 15 clapping 16 left 17 was 18 got back 19 opened 20 saw 21 were waiting 22 locked 23 shouted 24 came 25 tied 26 blindfolded 27 gagged 28 could hear 29 was talking 30 was saying 31 was saying 32 deserved 33 Deserved 34 did he mean 35 was going on 36 didn't someone tell 37 was happening

10b 1 happened 2 was 3 were all lying out 4 was reading 5 was just dozing 6 were looking for 7 arrived 8 was 9 looked 10 went 11 opened 12 thought 13 were 14 said 15 phoned 16 didn't answer 17 were you doing 18 heard 19 was having 20 couldn't 21 did you want 22 was clearing out 23 gave 24 came across 25 were addressed 26 all smelt 27 woke up 28 woke up 29 listened out 30 didn't hear 31 was snoring 32 were making 33 was dripping 34 opened 35 looked 36 was 37 was shining 38 thought 39 saw 40 could certainly hear 41 saw 42 was 43 was wearing 44 was hiding 45 ran

11a 1 has been 2 have filled 3 have always listened 4 have acted 5 have been interviewing 6 have you interviewed 7 have interviewed 8 have been talking 9 have been discussing 10 have had 11 have also been working 12 have been 13 have been circulating 14 have been seeing 15 have been learning 16 haven't learnt

11b 1 have you been doing 2 've been running 3 have you run 4 've been thinking 5 's been acting 6 's been crying 7 've been making 8 Have you talked 9 's said 10 have you been 11 've been talking 12 's been trying 13 've been 14 haven't heard 15 's had 16 's been 17 Has she broken 18 's been hurt

12a 1 haven't seen 2 met 3 have you been doing 4 've been doing 5 's been 6 've started 7 've been teaching 8 have finished 9 worked 10 enjoyed 11 wanted 12 've always enjoyed 13 thought 14 have you been 15 've done 16 've been working 17 've had 18 've given 19 's made 20 've done 21 've never had 22 worked 23 started 24 moved 25 was 26 did 27 was told 28 did you get 29 passed 30 've been doing 31 decided 32 couldn't get

12b 1 has just come in 2 has been 3 were 4 have been found 5 went 6 plunged 7 have now been informed 8 have set off 9 have not been given 10 were 11 has had 12 has somehow managed 13 have been 14 promised 15 was elected 16 has maintained 17 has claimed 18 has been 19 has ever had 20 came

13a 1 missed 2 did that happen 3 got 4 arrived 5 had just left 6 Did you have 7 was 8 arrived 9 knew 10 had forgotten 11 did she do 12 pretended 13 hadn't forgotten 14 said 15 wasn't 16 had got 17 was 18 had rained 19 was 20 smelt 21 were 22 had all gone 23 had arrived 24 had sat up 25 was 26 had only been

13b 1 sat 2 felt 3 didn't know 4 had gone in 5 had been 6 had looked 7 went in 8 felt 9 had already got 10 was 11 wanted 12 meant 13 had thought 14 had imagined 15 was 16 couldn't remember 17 had planned 18 almost decided 19 had to do 20 had spent 21 couldn't give up 22 were 23 felt 24 opened 25 had gone in 26 came out 27 smiled 28 hated 29 appeared 30 suddenly wished 31 had gone 32 got up 33 wondered 34 looked 35 felt

14 It was 10 o'clock at night. The offices of 'The Daily News' were buzzing with excitement. The deadline for the paper was in half an hour and they were frantically trying to finish the front page. Everyone had been working all evening without a break. Some of the journalists had been at the office since early morning. They had all been trying to get an exclusive story, to find out something that no other journalist had discovered. The main story was a big one. The Prime Minister had resigned. Everyone knew that his government had had lots of problems in the last year but his resignation was nonetheless a big surprise. Rumours had been going round all day about the real reasons for the announcement. Some said that he had been involved in some financial scandal. Others said that he had been seeing another woman. All the papers had been working all day to get the best story. And they had been doing their best to find out what the other papers had said. The whole day had been very tense. Suddenly the editor asked everyone to be quiet. There was a telephone call from the Prime Minister's office.

15 1 Are you coming 2 – 3 – 4 – 5 – 6 We're moving 7 – 8 – 9 I'm meeting 10 we're going 11 Are you going out 12 I'm not doing

16 1 'll buy 2 'll carry 3 will drop 4 Will you phone 5 will announce 6 Shall we tell 7 'll be 8 will receive 9 shall not/shan't invite 10 will be sentenced 11 will/shall never make 12 Shall we go 13 will not/won't offer 14 Shall I wash 15 shall have

17 1 are going to do 2 're going to have 3 're going to take 4 'll probably book into 5 Are you going to do 6 's coming 7 'll phone him up 8 're going to do 9 will be 10 're going to see 11 'll join 12 'll pick you up 13 Shall I bring 14 will make 15 will you bring 16 'll do 17 will save 18 are you going to see 19 're going to see 20 're going to try out 21 'll spend 22 'll see

18 1 leaves 2 arrive 3 get 4 will be shown 5 be given 6 is served 7 don't get 8 finishes 9 will be 10 are provided 11 is 12 will stay 13 will go back 14 are expected 15 find 16 will look 17 get back 18 will help 19 don't recognize 20 is served 21 is 22 plans 23 stay 24 won't be 25 get lost 26 will all have

19 1 'll be working 2 'll have to come over 3 'll talk 4 'll phone 5 Will you be 6 'll be recovering 7 Will you be going 8 'll give 9 'll be playing 10 'll be 11 'll pick you up 12 Will you be 13 'll be waiting 14 'll be doing 15 'll be doing 16 'll be living 17 'll still be working 18 'll probably be doing 19 won't 20 'll get 21 will 22 will 23 'll go 24 'll learn 25 won't be able to post 26 'll be going 27 'll take 28 'll give 29 'll be waiting 30 won't come 31 'll see 32 'll be carrying 33 'll have to get

20 1 Will you be seeing … will 2 are you going … 're going 3 'll be sitting 4 won't be walking … 's giving 5 are you doing … Are you going round … 'll be seeing 6 'll be going

21 1 will have heard … see 2 'll have finished … 'll give 3 will be … get in … 'll have been running around 4 will have been … 'll win 5 Will you have eaten … get … 'll make 6 won't have got … 'll probably get back 7 'll have finished … comes … 'll move in 8 'll be … see … 'll have been working 9 come … 'll have seen … 'll love 10 will have gone … 'll be

22 1 I'm about to go to work. 2 The Council intend to close the old swimming pool. 3 They are planning to have a big wedding in the summer. 4 The train is due to depart at 8.25. 5 The Condor Freight Company have agreed to provide free work clothes to all employees. 6 You are not to enter the building without signing your name in the register. 7 The Government have promised not to increase taxes during the next year. 8 The economy is on the point of collapse/collapsing. 9 The Department of Social Security has proposed cutting unemployment benefit. 10 My grandfather is about to die. 11 I hope to find a new job before the end of the year. 12 Do you promise not to tell anyone about this? 13 When do the two leaders intend to meet? 14 They are planning to move abroad. 15 You are due to arrive at the hotel at 7.30 in the evening.

23a 1 This information should have been given to us ages ago. 2 Do you want to be woken up in the morning? 3 I don't like being told what to do. 4 The windows are really dirty: they haven't been cleaned for weeks. 5 After being made redundant, he became very depressed. 6 I would like to have been given the chance to explain my point of view, but they weren't interested. 7 I'm hoping I'll be chosen for the college football team. 8 It is believed that many more people will die of skin cancer over the next ten years. 9 If it hadn't rained so much, the job would have been finished on time. 10 We can't take the car: it is being repaired (at the moment).

23b 1 The company is sorry to announce that it has been forced to introduce a range of cost-cutting measures as from the beginning of the new year. Unfortunately, free tea and coffee can no longer be provided. New coin-operated drinks machines are going to be installed in every department and a wide range of drinks can be purchased from these. Overtime payments will also be stopped after the end of this month and all members of staff will be expected to complete their duties within their contract hours. Personal calls must no longer be made from office phones and you are requested to use the pay phone in the basement for this purpose.

2 The Royal Hotel was almost completely destroyed by fire last night. By the time the Fire Brigade was/were called, the hotel was already blazing. Fifteen people were taken to hospital suffering from severe burns. Seven of them are said to be in a serious condition. (It is said that seven of them are in a serious condition.) The fire is thought to have been started by a discarded cigarette.

3 G: So, how was the holiday? J: Oh, it was fantastic. Everything was organized so well. As soon as we arrived at the airport, we were met and taken to the hotel. All the rooms had been beautifully cleaned and fresh flowers had been put on the tables. G: Oh, how lovely. And what about the food? J: It was excellent. It was all freshly prepared in the hotel and even the bread was made in the hotel kitchen. The bread rolls were served hot every morning with breakfast. G: Mm, it does sound good. I must say, I'd like my meals to be cooked for me for a couple of weeks. And what about the surrounding area? Was that nice? J: Oh beautiful. There were trips every day and we were shown all the local sights. There was so much history to see. You'd love it there, honestly.

4 Last month a plan was put forward (by the Council) to make the sea front traffic-free. The plan is supported by many of the shop and restaurant owners as they believe that their trade will be improved by a more pleasant environment. However, the hotel owners are less enthusiastic and say that access to their car parks will be made very difficult. There have also been protests from some local residents who complain that their journeys around the town will be made much longer.

23c 1 are being driven 2 are being killed 3 cross 4 are taken 5 are killed 6 make 7 often be seen 8 are hit 9 move around 10 be hypnotized 11 do not move 12 are sometimes hit 13 fly 14 Can anything be done 15 was built 16 have been constructed 17 lives 18 have been built 19 has been put up 20 look out 21 are often seen 22 be hoped 23 become

24 1 Why don't we have/get our picture taken? 2 I've finally decided to have/get my nose pierced. 3 We should have/get it repaired. 4 I'm afraid I haven't had my watch repaired yet. 5 We're going to have the kitchen redecorated next month. 6 If I were you, I'd have/get that tree felled. 7 I'm going to have/get them tested next week. 8 I love having my shoulders massaged. 9 I haven't had my teeth checked this year. 10 … she was having her hair washed. 11 I think he's had his hair dyed. 12 I haven't had all my work marked yet. 13 You must have/get it removed.

25 1 I wish I had a car. 2 I wish I hadn't gone to bed late last night. 3 I wish we lived in a nice big flat. 4 I wish I had bought that dress. 5 I wish he would stop shouting. 6 I wish I hadn't lost my temper. 7 I wish you had told me the truth. 8 I wish you would stop playing that music. 9 I wish I had gone to that concert. 10 I wish my job was/were more interesting. 11 I wish my family lived nearer to me. 12 I wish you would listen to me. 13 I wish I was/were with him now. 14 I wish I hadn't spent all my money on that new coat. 15 I wish we had eaten before we came out.

26a

Intransitive:	get on, go down, carry on, go up
Transitive: (separable)	take on, take off, put back, take up, fix up, give up, sort out

Transitive: (inseparable) get on with, come up to, look round for, run through, get away with

26b 1 Can we fix up a meeting soon? 2 You can't carry on going out every night. 3 I don't know how he gets away with it. 4 … we'll need to take on more staff soon. 5 We'll never get this problem sorted out if we don't talk about it. 6 The club membership has been going down for the last five years. 7 I'm going to take you off this case, detective. 8 I really think he should give up drinking. 9 It hasn't really come up to my expectations. 10 Her new job is taking up all her energy.

26c 1 was taken over 2 have put in for 3 have been turned down 4 have run out of 5 had saved up 6 fall back on 7 turns up 8 pick up 9 live off 10 come down 11 cheer me up 12 go on

27 1 had been … would have gone 2 don't tell … will regret 3 had come round … would have seen 4 happens … will lose 5 would help … had 6 loses … will resign 7 hadn't gone … would never have met 8 were … would use 9 gets … will be 10 would have been … had happened 11 break down … will be 12 knew … would help 13 would have married … had known 14 would be … spent 15 had … wouldn't moan

28 1 won't be allowed 2 didn't want 3 would advise 4 wanted 5 don't have 6 would have told 7 have 8 get 9 had phoned 10 come … tell 11 don't give 12 will be 13 would be called off 14 keep 15 would definitely come 16 had explained 17 would choose 18 might have understood 19 was/were 20 get

29 1 F 2 D 3 B 4 J 5 C 6 I 7 A 8 G 9 E 10 H

30 1 have been eating 2 won't want 3 took 4 would bring 5 are not collecting 6 'll go back 7 do 8 'll have finished 9 hadn't agreed 10 would have 11 hadn't taken on 12 wouldn't have 13 'll be lying 14 can get 15 get 16 don't see 17 have saved up 18 'll try 19 is 20 'll have saved up 21 haven't lost 22 had 23 would have left 24 keep on 25 'll be running 26 has been 27 haven't noticed 28 's still raining 29 've decided 30 hasn't phoned you up yet 31 don't tell

31 1 on condition that we pay him a reasonable fee 2 unless he asks me properly 3 If only I could get a job 4 Supposing that you had a lot of money 5 Assuming that the train arrives on time 6 What if he doesn't agree to my request? What will I do then? 7 as long as you get back by midnight 8 Imagine the helicopter hadn't been there to save her. What would have happened then? 9 Even if you'd offered to pay me a thousand pounds, 10 Provided that Rosie gets this new promotion,

32 1 Alison would make a very good managing director if she got the job. 2 I know that she could do really well if she worked hard/harder. 3 It would be horrible sitting out here if it wasn't/ weren't sunny. 4 He would not be able to live on his own if he didn't have the help of his neighbours. 5 We'll finish the job by the end of today if we're lucky. 6 You'll love it (in Indonesia) if you go there. 7 They may be imprisoned or even executed if they are deported. 8 The rain would have ruined them if you hadn't brought them in from outside. 9 I'm sure she would have forgiven him if he had told her the truth. 10 Many more would have died if they hadn't had the help of the Red Cross doctors.

33 1 I'll phone 2 he still couldn't read 3 We must leave 4 Can you come 5 You shouldn't/oughtn't to work 6 They might/could be 7 Shall we go 8 he would write 9 May I sit 10 He won't give 11 You needn't apologize. 12 May/Can I smoke 13 He could speak 14 I can't 15 I should/ought to stay in 16 she might/ could be 17 You mustn't tell 18 I will finish 19 Clare should/ought to be 20 He must be

34 1 can run 2 to be able to work 3 couldn't climb 4 could have died 5 be able to spend 6 can/could go 7 can be 8 can't understand 9 can't see 10 Being able to speak 11 couldn't say 12 couldn't phone her up … were able to get 13 could have done 14 haven't been able to sleep 15 couldn't put 16 be able to go out 17 Can you come 18 'll be able to ride 19 could be 20 could play

35 1 must have missed 2 can/may be exchanged 3 must be 4 will be 5 can't have moved 6 might be visiting 7 should/ought to do/have done 8 might/could be 9 can't still be playing 10 should/ought to have got 11 can be found 12 must be missing 13 might come 14 could/might have been 15 should/ought to have 16 will be … won't … 'll be having 17 might/could have been running 18 could/might be 19 can't have rained/can't have been raining 20 might join 21 must have been 22 should/ought to be expecting 23 should/ought to be 24 can't be 25 might have eaten … might/could have

36 1 had to leave 2 should/ought to offer 3 don't have to pay/needn't pay 4 haven't had to cook 5 must come round 6 had to run 7 shouldn't/oughtn't to have gone 8 do the prisoners have to be locked 9 shouldn't/oughtn't to be having 10 mustn't tell 11 shouldn't/oughtn't to allow 12 having to do 13 must go 14 doesn't have to get up 15 'll have to take 16 should/ought to have been working 17 should tell 18 needn't have bought 19 have to take 20 mustn't eat 21 don't have to come 22 must be hidden … must remain 23 Do you have to wear 24 needn't lie/don't have to lie 25 must follow

37 (One modal answer is provided here for each question but there are a number of possible answers for each one.) 1 Shall I open the door for you? 2 Would you answer the phone for me, please? 3 Would you like to go for a swim this morning? 4 Shall I make you a sandwich? 5 Could I make an appointment to see Ms Arnold, please? 6 You can use the phone if you want to. 7 Shall we go for a picnic this afternoon? 8 Would you wait here for me, please? 9 You can go out but you must be back before it gets dark. 10 Would you mind if I opened the window? 11 You can work outside today but you mustn't talk too much. 12 Shall I answer the phone? 13 Can I borrow a pen, please?

38 1 used to 2 used to/would 3 used to/would 4 used to 5 never used to/would never 6 used to/would 7 used to/would 8 often used to/would often 9 often used to/would often 10 used to 11 never used to/would never 12 used to 13 often used to/would often 14 used to 15 used to

39a Verb (+ person) + infinitive: arrange (for s.o.), decide, demand, expect, help (s.o.), hope, intend, invite (s.o.), learn, would like, manage, offer, plan, pretend, refuse, seem, want, wish

Verb + preposition + gerund: apologize for, approve of, discourage s.o. from, dream of/about, enquire about, insist on, learn about, look forward to, object to, succeed in

Verb + gerund: avoid, enjoy, finish, imagine, mind, miss

39b 1 to deliver 2 to stay 3 staying 4 to take 5 working 6 to be 7 getting 8 buying 9 smoking 10 to stay 11 talking 12 to stay in 13 not to leave 14 seeing 15 studying 16 living 17 upsetting 18 not keeping 19 to phone 20 to lock up

40 A: Megan, where were you last night? I tried <u>to find</u> you but I couldn't <u>see</u> you anywhere. James says he didn't <u>see</u> you <u>come</u> in to the party.

M: Yes Alex, that's right. I'm sorry. My parents wouldn't <u>let</u> me <u>come out</u> last night. I wanted <u>to see</u> you – honestly I did.

A: Why did your parents <u>make</u> you <u>stay in</u>? They usually <u>allow</u> you <u>to go out</u> in the evenings, don't they?

M: Yes, but I hadn't finished doing my homework. And they refused <u>to let</u> me <u>go out</u> until I had.

A: Oh dear, poor you. Oh well, never mind. Let's do something tonight instead.

M: OK. Actually, I'd <u>like to see</u> that new film.
A: Would you? I suppose it might be quite good but I'd rather just <u>go out</u> to the café. I was hoping <u>to have</u> a chance <u>to talk</u> to you properly.
M: Well, why not <u>do</u> both? We could <u>go</u> to the early showing of the film and then <u>go</u> to the café.
A: I'm not sure I can <u>afford to go</u> to the cinema.
M: That's all right. I've got some money.
A: So what time would you like <u>to meet</u>, then?
M: Six o'clock I suppose – in the cinema. I'll <u>try to get</u> there a bit earlier and <u>buy</u> the tickets.

41 1 I saw you cycling to work the other day. 2 I heard him leave the house early this morning. 3 She stood there and watched him drive away. 4 Did you notice me crying? 5 I've often seen you walking along the beach with your dog. 6 Have you ever heard him play (or playing) the saxophone. 7 I expect to find you working hard when I get back. 8 Did you hear me arrive? 9 I looked at the child smiling up at me and felt very sad. 10 We heard them arguing all night. 11 I can feel my hands shaking. 12 I watched you go to sleep and then I left. 13 I never really noticed your hair going grey. 14 I can smell smoke coming in through the windows. 15 He watches me play football every weekend.

42 1 to go out 2 to wash 3 to go 4 sending 5 going 6 trying 7 to inform 8 to apply 9 running 10 to consider 11 enrolling 12 waiting 13 to wait 14 to try 15 to find 16 acquiring/to acquire 17 to book 18 getting 19 to borrow 20 repairing 21 asking 22 buying 23 to give 24 walking 25 worrying 26 thinking

43a 1 from doing 2 about enrolling 3 about starting 4 of leaving 5 about cutting 6 on the neighbours helping 7 on paying 8 about losing 9 for not telling 10 of young people staying out 11 with writing 12 for starting 13 on living 14 against buying 15 on expanding

43b 1 finish 2 seeing 3 spending 4 see 5 do 6 speaking 7 get 8 working 9 finding 10 post 11 sleeping 12 working 13 give up 14 having 15 open

44 1 We're ready to leave. 2 He's afraid to tell her the truth. 3 I was delighted to receive your letter. 4 I was surprised to hear about their divorce. 5 It's rude to interrupt people. 6 It was very kind of you to bring those flowers. 7 It is very expensive to heat this house. 8 It was lovely to see you last night. 9 It is important to have interests outside work. 10 That child is very quick to learn.

45 1 to have 2 to see 3 to talk 4 to discuss 5 working 6 doing 7 to learn 8 to make 9 to say 10 welcoming 11 talking 12 giving 13 working 14 communicating 15 to see 16 to say 17 dealing 18 ensuring 19 Keeping 20 to do 21 being 22 failing 23 to carry out 24 to do 25 to work out 26 accepting 27 to do 28 apologizing 29 to calm down 30 to get 31 making 32 to do 33 to prove 34 to start 35 looking

46 1 to be chosen 2 Being accepted 3 to have kept 4 have been hiding 5 to be getting 6 saying/having said 7 getting/having got 8 to be living 9 being filmed 10 to have seen 11 to have left 12 taking part/having taken part 13 lying/having lied 14 to have resigned 15 being asked 16 to have finished 17 having been looked after 18 have been dancing/have danced 19 to have lost 20 being asked

47 1 She said (that) she would come and see us on Friday if that was all right. 2 The statement (said) that the conference would be spending a considerable time discussing the world debt crisis. 3 She explained (that) the shop was closing in about half an hour. 4 Gareth tells me (that) he's planning to set up his own business. 5 The managing director said (that) we/they were going to have to make quite a few cutbacks. 6 A spokesperson said (that) the police had been investigating new allegations of fraud. 7 She explained (that) when the project first started/had first started, there was/had been a lot of interest in it. 8 She told me (that) it was pouring with rain down there. 9 She promised me (that) she would have finished writing the report by the time I got there. 10 She says (that) her new computer has made a lot of difference to her. 11 The station announcer has just said (that) the 8.45 train from Waterloo will be arriving in approximately five minutes. 12 They told me (that) when they were setting up the organization, they had/had had very little money. 13 The treasurer told the meeting (that) the club had lost quite a lot of money last month/ the previous month. 14 He agreed (that) it would be a very difficult time for all of us/ them. 15 He told me (that) I worked too hard and that I should take more time off.

48 1 He asked me where I thought we should advertise. 2 Emma asked me if/whether I was going to audition for the play. 3 She told me to give her a ring if I needed any help. 4 She often asks me how you are getting on. 5 He's been wondering whether to ask her out for a meal. 6 He asked why Matthew had looked so embarassed when he saw Carole. 7 He asked if/whether we had to stay there all evening. 8 She wondered what they were doing about publicity for the event. 9 He asked me if/whether I would send him the report when it was finished. 10 She asked me what I had done with the student records. 11 She asked us if/whether we could keep our voices down a bit. 12 He wanted to know where I had bought the/that hat. 13 The doctor asked me if/ whether I had been eating properly.
14 They asked us not to make any noise during the perfomance. 15 Mike asked me if/whether I was still teaching music when I met Oliver.

49 1 He offered to help me type up the report.
2 He peruaded me not to hand in my resignation immediately. 3 He refused to discuss it with me. 4 He complained about not being invited/having been invited to the meeting. 5 The doctor advised him to take it easy for a few days.
6 The police warned him not to go near their house again. 7 The Ministry of Defence have decided to close down the naval base in two years' time. 8 She accused me of reading/having been reading her diary. 9 He reminded me to apply for a new passport. 10 She apologized for all the trouble she had caused.

50 *Model Answer*
In her acceptance speech, Diane Banham said that she was delighted to have been elected onto the Council and that she was very much looking forward to representing the interests of the residents of Kimbridge Valley. Having spoken to the many valley residents over the last few weeks, she said that she had a clear idea of the issues which were of most concern to them. The proposed closure of the school was understandably causing a great deal of anxiety and she hoped to be successful in fighting against that. She then thanked all her supporters and helpers.

51 1 I went to bed early so that/in order that I would be able to get up early. 2 It's an excellent course so I'm very lucky to get a place on it. 3 I don't really want to go to the cinema tonight because I can't afford it. 4 There is very little that the company can do about this since it is not their responsibility. 5 I've known her for a long time. However, I don't know much about her private life. 6 She's extremely generous, whereas her husband is the exact opposite. 7 Not only did I not say that: I didn't even think it. 8 The suspect is critically ill in hospital so/therefore we can't interview him for the time being. 9 I like working here because the people are very friendly. 10 (Either) I could do the work tonight or I could get up early in the morning to do it. 11 In a way, I both love the job and hate it. 12 He looks a bit overweight in spite of/despite being quite fit./He looks a bit overweight although he's quite fit./He looks a bit overweight. Nevertheless, he's quite fit. 13 Although the economy has been in recession all year, our sales have remained steady./The economy has been in recession all year; however,/nevertheless, our sales have remained steady./In spite of/Despite the economy being in recession all year, our sales have remained steady. 14 I've brought a photograph so that you can see how beautiful the place is. 15 The Government are getting worried because they're losing popularity. 16 I had a terrible headache last night so I couldn't go out. 17 My job is very interesting but/although it doesn't pay very well. 18 Either you leave now or I'll call the police.

52a A: Helen, I'm delighted to hear that you've decided to accept the post of junior manager.

H: Yes. I just hope that it turns out all right.

A: Oh, I'm sure it will. Is there anything in particular that you're worried about?

H: Well, yes. I'm not sure how the staff will respond to me as a manager. After all, I am quite a bit younger than most of them.

A: Oh, I wouldn't worry too much about that. I expect that some of them will be a bit hostile to you at first but they'll soon get used to the fact that you're the boss. It's important that you appear confident in your position, even if you don't feel very confident. The reason that you got this position at your age is that you're good and you must remember that.

H: Well, I hope that I will live up to your expectations of me. I will certainly try.

52b 1 I'm sure that he's lying to you. 2 What you did is unforgivable./It is unforgivable what you did. 3 She still holds on to the belief that he isn't dead. 4 We must be grateful for the fact that she hasn't made a complaint. 5 I don't know how many people are coming to the meeting. 6 The suggestion that she lied to you about it is ridiculous. 7 I presume that you're going with him. 8 Have you forgotten that Judith's coming round tonight? 9 I don't know if/whether she has passed her exams. 10 She is very angry about the fact that he didn't tell her the truth. 11 It remains doubtful if/whether she is good enough to do the job./If/whether she is good enough to do the job remains doubtful. 12 It is quite apparent that he has some emotional problems. 13 Have you arranged where we are going to meet tonight? 14 Do you know how she is? 15 I'm delighted that they're getting married.

53 1 I smelt something burning. 2 I went round to see her hoping for a reconciliation. 3 While hating the job, he did it for many years. 4 She came in looking furious. 5 Having plenty of time to spare, I had a good look round the town. 6 Wearing only a pair of shorts, he walked out into the darkness. 7 Having been out all day, I was quite happy to stay in for the evening. 8 The bedrooms overlooking the sea are the best ones in the hotel. 9 We're wasting time sitting here and doing nothing. 10 I have changed my job since last writing to you. 11 Before making a decision, I need to discuss it with my partner. 12 After having been friends for twenty years, we suddenly had a big argument and haven't seen each other since. 13 Having failed one of my exams, I couldn't get into university. 14 Loving her so much, he forgave her for everything. 15 I left them doing the washing-up.

54 1 Exhausted through lack of sleep, I fell asleep at my desk. 2 Abandoned by his parents at an early age, Peter took to stealing. 3 Although written many years ago, the book is still relevant today. 4 Since being promoted, I've had no time to go out. 5 Taken from his parents at an early age, the boy had a very difficult life. 6 Hidden in the cellar, the money was not discovered for many years. 7 Frequently criticized for his self-centred attitude, he was nonetheless very popular. 8 After being released from prison, Andy could not find a job anywhere. 9 Always dominated by the same people, the committee meetings were slow-moving and ineffectual. 10 On being caught, he confessed everything. 11 Seen from the outside, the building looks a mess, but it is lovely inside. 12 If elected, we will

increase the value of pensions.
13 Although ridiculed by everybody, he continued to pursue his bizarre projects. 14 Unless destroyed, this material could have damaging consequences. 15 Jennifer had been shoplifting for many years before being found out.

55a 1 as soon as I could 2 so that I can get my work done 3 as if/as though it was all my fault 4 as I'd hoped 5 as bad as you think they are 6 than your mother is now 7 although/whereas his father would like him to be a lawyer 8 so … that she never seems to do anything else 9 wherever you like 10 until I've seen it for myself 11 although/though/even though she can't find a job 12 Because/As/Since I didn't feel very well 13 so that no-one could find it 14 so/as long as/provided/providing that we don't stay late 15 Although/Though I like him

55b 1 Since 2 Although 3 as 4 even though 5 while 6 as if/as though 7 If 8 Since 9 however 10 so 11 than 12 If 13 wherever 14 unless 15 before 16 so that

56 Born in Holland in 1853, Vincent Van Gogh is one of the world's most famous painters. Although unrecognized throughout his life, his talent was much appreciated after his death.

Having failed in every career he had attempted, Van Gogh first turned to art to express his strong religious feelings. Having decided to become a painter, in about 1880, he started to paint studies of peasants and miners. During the next few years, known as his 'Dutch period', he produced paintings with rather dark greenish-brown colours.

In 1886, having gone to Paris to visit his brother Theo, he was immediately attracted to the Impressionist work he saw there. He decided to stay in Paris and continue his painting there. Encouraged by Pissaro to use more colour in his pictures, his subsequent paintings were bright and immensely colourful.

After moving/having moved to Arles in the south of France, in 1888, he worked frantically. This frenzied activity, interrupted by bouts of deep depression and despair, produced the majority of his most famous paintings. One of these, called Self Portrait with Bandaged Ear, shows Van Gogh wearing a bandage after having cut off his own ear. A year later, in 1890, he committed suicide.

A lot is known about Van Gogh's life and his feelings because of the hundreds of letters written by him to his brother Theo and others. Believing in Van Gogh's genius, his brother always encouraged him in his work. He was the closest person to Van Gogh.

57a 1 who killed Mr Makepeace (S) 2 who was staying in the room next door to him (S) 3 he owed her (O) 4 who always shared their table in the evenings (S) 5 who had murdered her husband (S) 6 that would be due to him from his father's life insurance policy (S) 7 he hates (O) 8 his mother is in love with (O) 9 she had married (O) 10 he had (O)

57b 1 She's the one I told you about. 2 I don't like the people who are staying with the Browns. 3 I like books that make you think about things. 4 I'm looking for the person whose car I've just hit. 5 Most of the books I read as a child are still popular today. 6 You can buy pasta from that Italian shop that has just opened in the high street. 7 The woman whose job I'm doing is coming back to work soon. 8 Is she the new television presenter everyone's talking about? 9 People who have a lot of leisure time often have very little money to spend on leisure. 10 Is Technico the company Sarah works for? 11 This is the job I've always wanted. 12 The swimming pool I use is only open to the public in the mornings. 13 We've just bought a computer package that teaches you how to play the piano. 14 My favourite holiday was the one we spent in a cottage in the mountains. 15 We haven't seen the friends that are coming to visit us this weekend for ten years.

58a 1 When I was in town, I met your sister, who was shopping for some clothes.

2 Their house, which is near the beach, needs a lot of work doing to it. 3 Sandra's just got a new job with Capital Insurers, which is a much better company than the last one she worked for. 4 The new manager, who/whom I met last week, seems to be a very capable woman.
5 This case, which I carried all the way from the station, is full of books. 6 The Games International Company, which we have done business with for many years/with which we have done business for many years, has just gone bankrupt.
7 The hospital, which is due to close down next year, has handed out redundancy notices to all its staff. 8 The prisoners, whose families are campaigning on their behalf, are requesting more time out of their cells. 9 The new government, which came to power with a lot of public support, is now facing major problems.
10 Her latest novel, which I read on holiday, is really good. 11 The Home Affairs Minister, who/whom the opposition has accused of lying, is suspected of being involved in a financial scandal. 12 The Education Department, which Mrs Parkinson is in charge of/of which Mrs Parkinson is in charge, is changing its policy on single sex schools.
13 The Lilley and Swan department store, which has a sale on at the moment, has made reductions on most of its goods.
14 The principal actor, who normally has a wonderful voice, could hardly speak last night due to a sore throat. 15 The sales manager, whose ideas I support, is planning a new advertising campaign.

58b 1 This new drug, which is very powerful, could have bad side effects.
2 Her father, who is staying in a nursing home, is said to be dying of cancer. 3 The Prime Minister, who is staying in his holiday home in Scotland at the moment, said that he was very saddened by the news of the air crash. 4 The story she gave, which her parents believed, was that she had not realised how late is was.
5 Agatha Christie, whose books are read all over the world, was a very prolific writer. 6 The sub-tropical gardens, which we love to walk round, are open all year.
7 The manager of the restaurant, who came over to apologize to us, said that she was very sorry about the undercooked fish. 8 Our Professor of Psychology, whose lectures I always attend, has written some very interesting books. 9 We packed a picnic and walked down to the beach, which was very crowded. 10 Next Saturday I'm going to visit my Aunty Sheila, who/whom I like very much.

59 1 with which the majority of soldiers went off to fight for their country.
2 who rushed to the enlistment centres
3 they had dug in the mud 4 who had been horribly injured 5 in which the image makers made an impact 6 which asked women to encourage their men to go to war 7 which seized the country
8 which gripped the nation 9 they had been told 10 which brutalized the people who took part 11 who put these feelings into words very effectively 12 who, in the poem Anthem for Doomed Youth, wrote 'What passing bells for these who die as cattle?' 13 who die as cattle 14 which described the horrific reality of war
15 who had not at first been anti-war
16 whose attitudes were changed by what they saw

60 1 The early morning is (the time) when I work best. 2 His mid-teens were the time when he first became interested in politics.
3 His dishonesty is (the reason) why I left him. 4 Edinburgh is (the city) where I'd most like to live. 5 The outdoor swimming pool, where we often went as children, has now been closed down.
6 This is a picture of (the place) where we're going for our holidays. 7 His refusal to tell her the truth is (the reason) why she is so angry with him. 8 This is (the place) where I fell off my bike. 9 The people I work with are (the reason) why I stay in the job. 10 That terrible night in December, when I found out what had been going on, changed my life forever.

61 1 You shouldn't listen to anything (that) he says. 2 It was nice to see all his family, most of whom I have met before. 3 The worst thing that can happen is that we'll miss the train. 4 I've read both the reports, neither of which I agree with. 5 The only thing (that) I need to do is to get some cash out of the bank. 6 The cleaners, several of whom have complained to me about their low pay, have decided to take industrial action. 7 Everything (that) I've done has been a failure. 8 I've lost any optimism that I once had for the future. 9 Members of the committee, many of whom are themselves suspected of corruption, have decided to call for an investigation. 10 The only thing (that) I can do is to give her the chance to talk about it. 11 Everyone who/that saw the argument said that Peter started it. 12 Those chocolates, half of which I've already eaten, were not meant to be for me. 13 The management team, none of whom I trust, are all saying the same thing. 14 The cheapest (that) I saw was about £5. 15 Her brothers, the youngest of whom is a friend of mine, have set up in business together.

62 1 She's going to have to sell the business, which is a great shame. 2 The weather's very cold at this time of year, which is why I don't go out very much. 3 He's decided to go and teach abroad, which will be an interesting experience for him. 4 They say he's been stealing money from the company, which is a terrible accusation to make. 5 She's going to have a month off work, which is just what she needs after all her problems. 6 He's going to give up his evening job, which will give him more time to spend with his girlfriend. 7 The editor has finally agreed to print an apology, which he should have done a long time ago. 8 She suddenly appeared on the doorstep last night, which was a complete surprise. 9 A few people have been attacked in this area recently, which is very worrying. 10 He's going to have an electric wheelchair soon, which will be a great help to him.

63a 1 hasn't it 2 have we 3 won't it 4 did you 5 won't it 6 shall we 7 is there 8 shall we 9 Are they 10 wouldn't you 11 did they 12 will you 13 isn't it 14 isn't it 15 wouldn't it 16 can we 17 could you 18 isn't it 19 doesn't it 20 Have you 21 did you 22 did you

63b D: Hello. Nice to see you here. It's a great party, **isn't it**?

T: Yes, it's really good, **isn't it**? There are so many people here that I haven't seen for ages.

D: Yes, there are a lot of our old school crowd here, **aren't there**? Have you spoken to many of them?

T: Yes, quite a few. I bumped into Adrian a few minutes ago and we had a brief chat. Well no, he chatted and I listened.

D: Yes, he's still the same, **isn't he**? He just loves talking about himself and he doesn't seem to be interested in what anyone else has to say, **does he**?

T: That's right. Oh look, that's Melanie over there, **isn't it**?

D: Yes, you're right, it is. Who's that she's with?

T: It's Matthew, **isn't it**?

D: But he's going out with her sister Emma, **isn't he**?

T: Well yes, I thought so. But he's holding Melanie's hand.

D: Oh yes. Well, I suppose our information must be out of date then, **mustn't it**? Anyway, what about you? I've missed you, you know.

T: Yes, I've missed you too.

D: But I expect you've got a new boyfriend now, **haven't you**?

T: Not now. I did for a little while after you went away but not now.

D: It was hard saying goodbye, **wasn't it**? I was going to write to you but I thought it wouldn't help.

T: No maybe not. Well anyway, we're here together now, **aren't we**? Why don't we just enjoy ourselves.

D: Good idea. Let's dance, **shall we**?

T: Yes, I'd like to. But not now. The music's terrible, **isn't it**?

D: Well it's no good for dancing, that's for sure. We'll go and ask them if we can change it, **shall we**?

T: OK. Well, you go. And put on one of our favourites, **will you**?

D: Yes, I will. And you will be waiting for me when I get back, **won't you**?

T: Yes, of course I will.

64 1 on 2 In 3 At/For 4 at/by 5 on 6 after 7 till/until 8 on 9 till/until 10 for 11 at 12 on 13 for 14 since 15 after 16 before 17 on

65 1 at 2 at 3 in 4 in 5 out of 6 on 7 out 8 to 9 from 10 to 11 to 12 from 13 to 14 on 15 onto 16 off 17 off/out of 18 into

66 1 on 2 in 3 in 4 until/till 5 in 6 out of 7 to 8 on 9 in 10 for 11 since 12 before 13 to 14 after 15 from 16 for 17 to/till/until 18 Since 19 On 20 at 21 at 22 before 23 for 24 after 25 on 26 on 27 into 28 before 29 as 30 before 31 in 32 onto 33 into

TEST 1

Part A

1 –
2 a
3 the
4 the
5 –
6 –
7 the
8 a
9 the
10 the

Part B

1 She bought a lovely new silk blouse.
2 The shop sells expensive old handmade objects.
3 She seldom gets to work before 9.00.
4 I'll probably see him early in the morning when I come to work. *or* I'll probably see him when I come to work early in the morning.
5 He left the house quite suddenly after his phone call.

Part C

1 more interesting
2 harder
3 better
4 more spacious
5 quieter
6 friendlier
7 more difficult
8 the newest
9 harder
10 easier

Part D

1 did you work
2 left
3 Have you met
4 've known
5 's
6 've been going
7 Has the phone rung
8 was cooking
9 didn't answer
10 'd already left

Part E

1 're taking (are going to take)
2 's going to
3 'll
4 stay
5 'll call

Part F

1 He got the job despite not having much experience.
2 She was quite nervous, so she didn't do very well.
3 He seems well-educated; however, he's not very bright.
4 I hired him because he had so much experience.
5 She is not only beautiful and intelligent but kind and thoughtful.

Part G

1 onto
2 to
3 During
4 after
5 until

TEST 2

Part A

1 will have been working
2 will have to finish
3 not to speak
4 Will you be waiting
5 don't intend to marry
6 will do
7 didn't come

8 wrote
9 had known
10 would stop

Part B

1 has just come in
2 was broken into
3 was forced
4 were shattered
5 left
6 told
7 was taken/had been taken
8 to be repaired
9 are working
10 to be made

Part C

1 turned it down
2 takes after
3 come up with
4 gave it up
5 run out of

Part D

1 to express
2 typing
3 to use
4 working
5 to meet
6 working
7 to be
8 to further
9 working
10 hearing

Part E

1 He wore himself out hiking all day.
2 After having heard/hearing the news, we came over as quickly as possible.
3 Having worked hard all day, she wanted to go out for dinner.
4 Soon after moving up north, he regretted his decision.
5 While sympathizing with your point of view, I cannot totally agree with you.

Part F

1 That's the woman whose dog bit me.
2 Can you tell me about the town where you were born?
3 I found the book which/that was taken from the library.
4 I can't remember when I first heard that song.
5 The woman who married my best friend is my cousin.

Part G

1 have you
2 could she
3 did you
4 didn't it
5 are they

TEST 3

Part A

1 finished
2 would have died
3 wouldn't go
4 isn't
5 go
6 get
7 wouldn't have hit
8 won't come
9 were
10 had been

Part B

1 e
2 d
3 h
4 f
5 a
6 i
7 j
8 c
9 g
10 b

Part C

1 I think this umbrella **could/must** be Emily's ...
2 After I've been studying French for another year, I **will be able to speak** it more fluently.
3 We **must leave** as soon as she gets here.
4 You ought **to** write to your parents more often.
5 He **can't be** very bright ...
6 I wish I **could** come to your party.

7 He must **wait** until the bank opens.
8 They'll have to **take** …
9 … I **can** stay out until midnight.
10 May I **use** this phone to make a private call?

Part D

1 mustn't
2 shouldn't
3 need to
4 needn't
5 should

Part E

1 to be chosen
2 having done
3 having lied
4 to have completed
5 to be doing

Part F

1 was going to resign
2 hadn't realised
3 would be
4 had caused
5 had been playing
6 wasn't
7 had completely forgotten
8 are having/were having
9 would have been working/will have been working
10 didn't have